Unspeakable Joy

To Judy Perry

[handwritten inscription]

[signature]

For my long-suffering mother

Unspeakable Joy

Fred Moody

...otherwise Mikheev would immediately tumble into the grass and flowers, spilling all the letters as he did so. They would be caught up by the wind and taken across the river, into the backwater meadows....

—Sasha Sokolov

Table of Contents

Unspeakable Joy

1

Bless me Father, for I have sinned. It has been forty-four years since my last confession.

Δ

So. What happened was, I got a call from my mom—the first and still the only time she ever called me at work.

As soon as I answered, she burst into tears and started raving incoherently. This was wildly out of character—she was not what you would call a demonstrative woman.

I couldn't figure out what was wrong until she finally calmed down enough to tell me it was something she'd seen on a TV news program just before she called. She'd been half-listening to the usual news, politics, national stuff—until they suddenly got her full attention when they started reporting on priests sexually abusing students in a Catholic seminary.

Δ

Old news by now, I know, but this was the first of these stories of ongoing widespread abuse in the Church to come out. Some kid had gone to the police in 1992 and told them what happened to him in his seminary, and when the investigation actually got somewhere and the story broke a year later—the story my mom was watching on TV—it turned out to be a legitimate shocker: sexual abuse of boys had been going on in this place since the 1960s, without anyone ever saying a thing. It was like the Franciscans who ran the institution had quietly got the word out around the world to likeminded friars that this was the place where lovely little flowers of St. Francis were ripe for the plucking, and they'd all managed to find their way there. By the time they were outed, eleven different priests had abused hundreds of boys for a good twenty-seven years. And not once had any of the abusers run any risk of being discovered.

But that wasn't the worst of it, as far as my mom was concerned. What sent her over the edge was the name of this seminary: St. Anthony's, in Santa Barbara. I'd been a seminarian in that place, back in the late 1960s, when the first known abuser was happily at work there.

Good old Father Mario. Blessings be upon him.

Δ

It didn't help that Mom had such vivid memories of the state I was in when I came home from St. Anthony's in 1967, during my senior year. I'd transferred there from my previous seminary (a transfer, it turned out, from the twentieth back to the fourteenth century), and only lasted five months. She was a juvenile probation officer then, and knew how to recognize the signs of sexual abuse in kids: withdrawal, depression, low self-esteem, etc. etc. etc.—a list that matched up nicely with the symptoms I brought home with me.

Δ

Here's the kind of conversation we would routinely have in those first post-seminary months, during which I pretty much just hid in my room, leaving the house only to go to school or church:

Mom: "Why don't you take the car this Friday and take a nice girl to the prom?"

Me: "No nice girl would want to have anything to do with me!"

Δ

It wasn't even imaginable in those days, sexual abuse of children by priests, so she didn't have any suspicions about it at the time. But now, living in a completely different world, watching this story come out, she put two and two together and called me in tears, screaming, "Were you one of the victims? Were you one of the victims?"

I felt terrible for her—she'd sent me, her oldest child, off to a distant seminary when I was only fourteen, and it wasn't until I became a parent myself that I could begin to understand how agonizing that had to have been for her. And now this nightmare.

"It's OK, Mom…I wasn't. Nothing like that ever happened to me—honest. You really have to not worry about that. It never happened to me—never."

Δ

Mom's travails made for quite a contrast with the kind of thing I used to read in my first seminary's monthly student newsletter, *The Coastline*, back in 1963:

MOTHER OF A PRIEST
By Mike Hogan

The greatest earthly joy that a human mother could experience was possessed recently by Mrs. Eberhard. I once read a poem that portrays very beautifully the feelings of a mother on her son's ordination day. I don't think I shall ever forget it. All the results of years of sufferings, joys, trials, and teachings have now blossomed forth into not only a strong young man but a representative of Christ as a priest.

There is an unspeakable joy in a mother's heart as her son, now a grown man who seemingly yesterday was just a boy steps up to the bishop. At this solemn moment, her warm and loving heart stops as though it would beat no more. The bishop slowly dips his finger into the oil and anoints that young man a priest. As tears stream down her cheeks and her heart bursts with joy, she silently says a prayer of thanks to God. Her son, now a priest, tenderly turns his mind to his mother. All of her sweet caresses in time of trouble and her stern lectures in time of need; all these flash before his mind as small, glistening diamonds eternally embedded in her crown of glory. Her many emotions can be summed up in these beautiful words: "Today I see my dreams and hopes fulfilled, today I am the mother of a priest."

2

When you live with a secret, you'd think it would fade with time. But it doesn't; instead, it just endures, keeps growing more vivid, strengthening its hold on you, turning into an ever-worsening problem the more time goes on and the more you accrue the trappings and track record of a normal life—all of which I had in spades by the time that call came.

Marriage, kids, house, friends, career…when you're like me, those things are basically barnacles on a rotting pier.

I suppose, for the secretive, the power of the secret has some direct correlation with the worth of the life you have: the more loved ones in your life, the more emotional equity, the more you have to lose by being found out. The best you can manage is the occasional short period of relative sanity when you almost forget and just kind of cruise along until something either inside or outside you throws the whole thing right back in your face. Then you feel like a complete moron for having allowed yourself to think you could keep on living the I'm-a-normal-person lie.

Δ

On the other hand, the truth about that place, and about me being in it, is as indescribable now as it was unlivable then. How the hell do you talk to mentally healthy people about it? You can tell from the look they get on their face as soon as you mention it that they think the whole topic is icky—and that's before they even hear any specifics. Like about how once when I was sixteen, when our Spiritual Director found me sitting outside in the middle of the night, depressed, invited me into his office to talk, served me my first-ever alcoholic drink—Kahlua—then took me down to the monastery to say a private Mass on the main altar, during which he whispered in my ear at the Kiss of Peace, "I love you, you fool."

Δ

Or how when I was Sports Prefect and working with my best friend (my "particular friend," if you will), down on the ballfields one hot day, and he suddenly stripped off his shirt, setting off a reaction in me that I recognized as sexual, leaving me guilt-ridden and horrified for months. And never able, out of shame, to bring it up in Confession, thereby compounding the sin.

Δ

So whenever some conversation required me to account for my high-school years, I would just say I'd gone to "a boarding school in California" and hope no one would ask any questions about it. If I had to say that I'd been in a seminary, the first thing people would want to talk about was celibacy and how I could possibly have thought I wanted to live such a freakish life.

Δ

This was back in those halcyon days of innocence when celibacy was the first thing people thought of when they thought about priests. Now, when people find out you were in a seminary, all they want to know is whether you were some panting priest's catamite. And when you say you weren't, you can't help but feel they don't believe you, that they fear you're damaged in some way, possibly dangerous.

3

I got Mom calmed down, but I had a feeling she'd be calling again—God only knew what they were going to uncover once they got started on this story. It would just be one dismal revelation after another.

All I could think about at first was how it would be impossible for reporters now to get any idea at all what it was like back then in those places. You could already tell that was the case by how baffled they were at how no one ever reported this abuse to anyone, for all those years. To them—the reporters—it just didn't make any sense that priests raping and sodomizing and otherwise sexually abusing boys in a Catholic seminary would go completely undetected year after year after year. But to me, it made perfect sense, that prodigious, uniquely Catholic capacity for repression. And the story coming out now suddenly made all these strange memories I had from back then—memories of indecipherable, mysteriously disturbing events—make perfect sense as well.

Fred Moody

4

As a lapsed Catholic and particularly as an ex-seminarian, you have no appreciation for the dimensions of your own weirdness until some chance episode throws it into bold relief. Like when I went to a psychiatrist—the second in a series over fifteen years or so—seven years after having left the seminary. I was trying to deal with crippling depression and self-loathing, festooned by endless dreams and nightmares that were always set in ruined cathedrals. I took a battery of tests, drew a self-portrait, told the doctor why I was there, and finally there commenced the inevitable recitation of my life story, which included my having been in a seminary.

My description of the institution freaked the psychiatrist out. He'd been politely listening and taking notes until I got to talking about it. Then he suddenly sat up straight and started peppering me with questions, finally culminating with—and I have no idea what brought him to this one—"Didn't you ever masturbate?" When I said, truthfully, "No," he slumped down in his chair, looking utterly defeated.

Δ

The strangest thing about that experience was that it left me wondering why he thought my answer was so weird. I felt that I should know—that it should be obvious—and my confusion only served to make me feel all the weirder. Like I was disconnected from myself, not able to feel my own feelings, connect with my own unhappiness.

Δ

Eventually, the psychiatrist became fixated on what he saw as my "anger problem." Even though I had never brought up anything about "anger." Since I never felt particularly angry about anything, or at anyone, this was pretty much the last thing I ever expected to come out of these sessions. But he just went on and on about it, how "angry" I was. So I came more and more to doubt his abilities—even his sanity—and finally just quit going to him.

Δ

I don't know, though. It's funny how you never remember things when you should. Like during the year I took off between undergrad and grad school, when I was working as a bank messenger and playing on the bank's basketball team. A neighbor, a new friend I'd made, played for an opposing team, and we played against each other in the season's first game. I remember right at the beginning of the game fighting for a rebound that my team got, then turning to run upcourt with my teammates and hearing a tremendous crash to the floor behind me. I knew without looking that it was my friend, but I didn't know what had happened to him.

My wife, who was there watching, told me afterwards that I'd cold-cocked him with a vicious elbow to the side of his head. On purpose. She said it was "scary." And that my friend looked up from the floor, completely bewildered, like he couldn't believe I'd really done what I'd done.

But even after being told, I had absolutely no memory of having done it, and no matter how hard I tried, not only couldn't I conjure it up—I couldn't even remember feeling the tiniest bit pissed off.

I should have remembered that story when the psychiatrist was going on and on like he was about my "anger." The basketball incident had happened only a few months before and was a perfect example of what he was talking about—how I couldn't connect with this rage or whatever inside me.

But the story just didn't come to mind at the time. And it's only now that I'm making the connection. And remembering too how whenever I played sports—basketball, tennis, softball—in those adult leagues during those years, I was constantly losing my temper in a way I never did anywhere else. Along with that weird kind of blackout. I never really got over that, either, until I quit playing.

5

All of us in the seminary, whether from Washington, Oregon, Idaho, Montana, or California, came from essentially the same place: a deliberately isolated Catholic community, with its own school, in either a small town or a suburb. We were as separate in our way from the rest of the world as the Amish are now. School uniforms; Mass in Latin every Sunday without fail, and with fasting from the previous midnight; calendars with every day devoted to a particular saint or God-related event; confession every week, at a minimum; no meat on Fridays; that big splashy morbid display on the forehead every Ash Wednesday; extra observances during Lent, featuring daily Stations of the Cross; constant recitation of the Rosary, with its three sets of Mysteries; little prayerful ejaculations—"All for the love of Jesus, through Mary with a smile" being my personal favorite—uttered throughout the day; and on and on and on, always something to set you apart from the flawed, the fallen.

(Yes, they really were called "ejaculations.")

And within that separate community were kids like me, yet another degree removed from the outside world. None of us headed for the seminary in those days were what you would call mainstream.

Δ

It was with the onset of puberty that you began
to feel this profound estrangement from the surrounding
community of regular Catholics. I suppose my first overt
step toward that estrangement—that is, the moment when
I first really felt marked as different, destined for a life apart
from humanity—came in fourth grade, when the nuns at
Assumption School treated us to an afternoon movie in the
cafeteria. The movie was some Shirley Temple classic with
a scene where Shirley Temple undresses for bed by backing
up to a bedpost and sliding down it in a way that makes
her shirt come off. I hurriedly closed my eyes and bowed
my head when I saw what was about to happen, and when
I opened them I saw my classmate David Harris staring at
me with a mocking expression, shaking his head.

Why was I like that? Even the other Catholics
thought I was strange. I hated being that way—was deeply
ashamed of it, in fact—but at the same time I couldn't help
myself.

Δ

All through those last years at Assumption, fifth
through eighth grade, this unendurable unease would come
over me whenever any friends or classmates talked about
girls' emerging attributes: Caroline Sands's ass, Terri Mac-
Millan's tits…this kind of talk, which seemed to be constant, always sent me into a weird tailspin of fear, shame,
depression. The fear was instinctive, reaction to powerful feelings I couldn't define or even identify. I would be
ashamed alternately at my discomfiture and my inability
to rebuke my fellow boys for the egregious sin of speaking
so rudely and disrespectfully about friends and classmates

who happened to be girls. It didn't help that I was already mortified over my privately having noticed Caroline Sands's ass and Terri MacMillan's tits, and had come to think that I was a monster for thinking about them all the time. Week after week, I would go traipsing off to confession to whisper frantically that I'd had "bad thoughts" about Caroline Sands and Terri MacMillan, and hope against hope that this time the confession and the penance meted out would somehow make my problem go away.

I always ended up fading to the fringe of the group when this kind of talk started, hoping that no one would notice my inability to join the fun. And I would settle every time on the notion that something was deeply wrong with me.

Δ

The end result of this madness generally had people like me figuring out early on—in my case, by fifth grade— that we weren't destined for normal lives. So by default we began thinking about the seminary, which you entered at the beginning of ninth grade, at age fourteen. Surely this constant unease, this growing estrangement, and especially this terrible reverence for girls, this fear of talking to them, all amounted to a sign from God, a calling (a conviction that grew stronger along with the parish priest's growing affection for you). Nothing else could explain our weirdness but that we were chosen, set apart, called to a vocation inaccessible to normal people.

Δ

So we became devoted altar boys and started hang-

fornia, with its legendary weather, surf music, white Levis, and overall hipness, was the nation's teen paradise.

Δ

But to be honest, the first thing that came to mind whenever I looked forward to seminary life was that there would be no girls there. If I had considered the reality of entering a seminary in any other light, it's hard to believe I'd have found the idea sane, let alone enticing: You entered at age fourteen, spent six years in a "minor seminary," then another six years (if you made it that far) in a "major seminary," then re-entered the world at age twenty-six, formed into an entirely different person, having sequestered yourself until adolescence was safely over.

Crazy, I know. But it seemed like a good idea at the time.

I had no idea why, but my terror of girls was such that the only hope I saw for myself was to carve out a life where I wouldn't have to have anything to do with them. It trumped every other consideration. And the priesthood offered not only that opportunity in the form of a calling to celibacy, but a hefty serving of admiration over my "sacrifice" as well.

I took on a freakish religiosity, going to Mass every morning before school, often serving as altar boy, and frequently serving all three masses on Sunday. And I suppose I was never happier than when I was serving Mass, or laying out the priest's vestments beforehand, or simply alone in the church, playing at meditation and prayer. But it all had more to do with the place being a sanctuary than for any kind of genuinely religious experience I was having there. If I'd been able to admit that to myself at the time, I'd have been spared no end of misery.

Δ

Which is not to say that I had any idea about this at the time. I believed fervently that was born for a life of intense religious devotion, and I looked constantly for signs of danger, for signs that my devotion was faltering, so as to forestall any decline in my religiosity, my worthiness.

I was particularly obsessed as the time drew near for the visit by the priest who'd be interviewing me to determine my suitability for Holy Redeemer. My mother took me to our little downtown department store, The Golden Rule, to help me buy something to wear for the interview. We settled on a black cardigan sweater that would go nicely with my school-uniform salt-and-pepper cords.

I tried it on, looked for a long time at my reflection in the mirror, grew increasingly nervous, then asked Mom: "Do you think I look too worldly in this sweater?"

7

It was a two-hour drive from our Bellingham home to the King Street Station, in Seattle, where I was to board my train to Oakland and the seminary. I was fourteen; it was early September, 1963. I was excited not only to be on my way after an eternity of waiting, but to finally be meeting my own kind. I was to rendezvous with four other new seminarians, then the train would gradually take on more newcomers and upperclassmen as we made our way south on the rail line. By the time we got to Oakland, we filled an entire car.

I still have a picture my mom took of the five of us in that first group, standing beside the train we're about to board. It's a tangible reminder of the beginning of my disillusionment, for it was clear at the outset that the other four weren't so much fellow religious adepts as fellow losers. In the picture, we make a collective grotesque: one of us (me) comically skinny, a legitimate geek; another short and fat, with buck teeth and horn-rimmed glasses; a third looking like Baby Huey; the fourth, another skinny kid, with the haunted look of someone long accustomed to getting beaten up at school; and the fifth a nondescript dork with the requisite high-waist pants. Most of us were in brand-new clothes and all five of us looked like our hair had been cut by our dads. (Mine, in truth, had been.)

Once aboard, I shrunk down in my seat, against a window, and tried to tune out the whole lamentable spectacle unfolding in our car. Before long, it would be packed with misfits sporting bad clothes, misshapen bodies, bad haircuts, geeky glasses, pimples, crooked teeth. We were like a shipment of flawed children sent off by our embarrassed parents to a distant location, to be put safely out of sight.

By the time we left Portland for the overnight leg to Oakland, the car was full, it was getting dark outside, and the upperclassmen were smoking cigarettes and getting down to the business of getting drunk.

Δ

I managed a little sleep off and on, checking anxiously for my ticket in between naps, and awoke finally to a view of the sun rising into the bluest sky I'd ever seen, over an endless and glorious landscape of plowed black earth giving off steam. I had left Seattle on a cold and cloudy day, and now was waking to mythical beauty and warmth. *California.*

I was drawn out of my reverie by an upperclassman who sat down in the seat opposite. His name was Dick Libby, and he stood out from the group because he was cool.

He was concerned, it turned out, about my obvious horror at what I'd seen and prayed over the night before. "You rookies"—this was the first time I'd heard the seminary term for freshmen—"should try not to get the wrong impression from what was going on last night. That wasn't the norm for us...for seminarians ...at all. It was an exception, really." His effort was undercut by his still being visibly drunk, with blood-shot eyes, a tongue tied in knots, and the air of someone navigating familiar territory. "I just don't want you to be dish...dil...dist...dishillusioned!" He couldn't get the word to come out right—a morning condition I'd seen over the years in Dear Old Dad.

Δ

I didn't know a soul and it seemed like everybody else on the train had friends. The conversation with Libby was the only conversation I had during the entire ride. I was painfully aware that no one was talking to me, introducing himself, or offering to befriend or even guide me to the seminary once we reached Oakland. There wasn't a hint of religiosity in this crowd, either—most of the upperclassmen looked like ungainly versions of the bullying kids I'd always feared and tried to avoid, rather than the kindred spirits I'd been expecting.

So instead of steaming toward a new life in a state of high excitement, I was lapsing into my customary state of self-pitying isolation.

We arrived; I noticed an upperclassman who didn't seem to have any friends. He had greasy hair, huge eyeglasses, and the biggest Adam's apple I've ever seen. I had heard people calling him, variously, Richard, Ree-shard, and Retard, always in a mocking tone.

I worked up the nerve to ask if I could tag along with him so I wouldn't get lost between the station and the seminary, and he nodded yes. There didn't seem to be any organized way to get there. I followed him to where we watched our luggage get loaded onto an old truck with the seminary's name painted on its doors. It was driven by a young priest in a Redemptorist habit. Once we saw our bags safely loaded, we took off, me following him down the street leading out of the station.

Δ

Somehow we ended up over in San Francisco, in Chinatown. We walked into a store full of scarves, fans, and other stuff I took to be "Chinese." We stopped at a table in the middle of the store and started rummaging through things. I picked up a pack of cards and turned one card over to see a picture of a nude woman. I looked at two or three more, then put the pack down, scandalized. I looked up at Richard, who was looking through a similar pack. Gathering evidence, I thought; I kept waiting for him to throw the pack down and confront the store owners—kind of a Jesus throwing the moneychangers out of the temple moment.

But he didn't. Instead, he went through the cards slowly, one by one, until he'd seen them all. There was no question but that he was taking pleasure in them.

I kept looking back and forth between Richard and the woman behind the counter—a little demure middle-aged Chinese woman with glasses, the picture of modesty and propriety—and feeling myself coming completely unmoored from everything I believed to be true.

Δ

But I didn't say a word—not to Richard, not to the woman behind the counter. Thus began my inexorable slide from grace, the first in an endless series of moral compromises of a kind I'd thought impossible for seminarians.

Fred Moody

8

By the time I entered the seminary gates that evening, I was thoroughly disillusioned. But I'd also decided not to tell my parents what this place was really like. Even though I was scared, and had already discovered that it wasn't at all what I expected, I didn't want to have to go back home.

Δ

I had long known, after all, that people are "whited sepulchres"—a truth I first learned in grade school, from Matthew 23:27: "Woe unto you, scribes and Pharisees, hypocrites! for ye are like unto whited sepulchres, which indeed appear beautiful outward, but are within full of bones of the dead, and of all uncleanness." This metaphor was trotted out in religion classes and sermons throughout my childhood, and it seized my imagination more than anything I was ever taught. (The Stigmata was a close second.) I would constantly picture myself all clean and normal on the outside, going about my daily routine, surrounded by people who thought nothing out of the ordinary about me, while my insides were the slimy, dripping interior of a tomb, or a pile of writhing maggots, or full of rotting flesh and bones—reeking, stinking, foul in any case.

Δ

I still have this problem—a reflexive, shame-driven tendency to secrecy. I'm convinced that anything I'm thinking or feeling—the inside of the sepulchre—will disgust my friends, my family, my bosses, co-workers...whoever.

Exactly the way I was with my parents about the seminary, never even hinting to them what the place (me in that place) was really like. I was a completely different person there from the one I was at home and I've carried that divided sense—that sense of being a chameleon defined by the place and people around me, that sense of secretly being someone else no matter where I am—everywhere I've been. I've come to think of it as a fundamentally Catholic reflex.

Δ

And like with this writing—I don't want anyone to know what it is. My wife keeps asking me about it, wanting to see it, and I won't show it to her, won't tell her anything at all about it. "Is it fiction or nonfiction?" she asks. "I'm still thinking about it," I answer.

Fred Moody

9

We were awakened every morning by the clanging of a handheld bell. The Father ringing it would intone, "Tu autem, Domine, miserere nobis," and we would respond, "Deo Gratias."

A half-hour or so later, after ablutions, we'd go to Chapel in Silence, for morning meditation, which was followed by Mass, followed by breakfast. After we said Grace at breakfast, the Father in charge would ring another hand-held bell, and we would break our Silence with this explosion of sound, everybody starting to talk at once.

Meditation, Mass, breakfast, classes, lunch, classes, work period, recreation, supper, study hall, evening prayers, resumption of Silence, bed. There was something undeniably comforting about it, the routine. The only sound in the dorm, after lights out: the rhythmic clicking of Fr. Simpson's rosary as he strode up and down the aisles between the rows of bunk beds.

Δ

Silence was always characterized by people trying to get some hapless soul to break it. So you'd always see certain wags making faces at a classmate, trying to get him to laugh out loud, or goosing, tickling, punching a victim, trying to elicit noise. Endless jostling, angry leave-me-alone glares, looks of patient long-suffering.

Δ

We didn't wear uniforms or habits, but we did get these really cool jackets that looked like varsity letterman's jackets: made of felt, with snaps down the front, an "HRC" and a cross sewn on where the athlete's letter would be, and sleeves that I took to be leather, although they probably were some kind of vinyl. I kept those sleeves clean by frequently, and lovingly, washing them with saddle soap. We all wore them every day unless it was too hot outside. They were a kind of uniform. I felt very cool when I had mine on, even though it fit me like the shell from a much larger beast.

Much as I loved it, though, I never wore it off the seminary grounds.

Δ

Food was cooked in the refectory kitchen by an order of nuns from eastern Europe, who did all of our cooking and cleaning. They were the hardest-working people I've ever seen. As far as I could tell, none of them spoke English. There were four of them, all elderly—stout, hapless souls who lived in a little decrepit house out at the far end of the seminary's playfields. They were like characters in a children's story—anthromorphized potatoes dressed in habits.

At meals, they would start sliding trays and pitchers of food and drink through an opening between the kitchen and refectory as soon as we'd said Grace and Father had rung the Silence-ending bell. When all the food had been passed through, they would slide the door down, closing off the passage.

We sat eight to a table, at eleven tables, with roughly the same mix of classes at each: one sixth- or fifth-year student, who sat at the table's head; one fourth-year student; one or two juniors; one or two sophomores; two or three rookies at the foot of the table. Each class was considerably smaller than the one behind it; as the year wore on, more seminarians would leave and their chairs would remain empty for the rest of the year—a constant reminder of how difficult it was to make it all the way through to ordination.

You entered through a door in one corner of the room, off the covered walkway from chapel. To your left, against the wall, was a platform with a podium and a table and chair on it for the Father who supervised the meal; next to that was a gigantic toaster, roughly the size of a tabernacle; and in the corner beyond was the hatch to the kitchen.

Breakfast generally consisted of a pitcher of hot chocolate made with water; a pitcher of milk; bowls of oatmeal—shiny, lumpy, kind of slimy; trays of rubbery, tepid pancakes; and toast. The platters and pitchers were made of metal; at dinner and supper, the hot chocolate was replaced with a Kool-Aid-like drink that everyone called "bug juice."

None of this was particularly appetizing—all anyone ever really wanted to eat was the toast, production of which was highly ritualized and competitive, and undertaken by the seminarians rather than the sisters.

Δ

Toast at breakfast was arguably the greatest licit pleasure the seminary had to offer. For most of us, it was an obsession—there was something unsettlingly sinful about the way we planned for it, prepared for it, devoured it.

Each night just before lights out, the head of each table would track down one of his table's rookies to tell him that he was to be next morning's toast maker. It was a big responsibility: after Mass, while the rest of the seminarians were shuffling in a line to the refectory, the rookies assigned to toast-making would rush ahead, still observing the Silence, jostling one another for position, and get in line at the toaster. The first in line would start in immediately making toast before Grace had even started.

It was vital to follow procedure exactly. The loaves of bread stacked next to the toaster came in a shiny reinforced paper wrapper that tore easily and neatly, and you would pop the wrapper open exactly in the middle, cutting three of the four sides so that you could fold the package open, making two even stacks of bread to be toasted. Then you would put slices of bread, two at a time, on racks that ascended into the toaster and carried the slices through, depositing them at the bottom after they'd been toasted. You would put the toasted slices back in the wrapper, and when it was full you would take the package, re-closed to keep in warmth, to your table.

The whole time you were doing this, your tablemates would be anxiously watching—first to see where you were in the line, then to see how soon you'd be delivering the goods.

Δ

Each table got one full loaf. At table, the toast was served in descending class order, with the slices in the middle of the loaf being the most prized because they were the hottest and least soggy. Each of us got three slices, and you could trade favors of one kind or another (work, homework, treats sent from home) for more. The general method of ingestion was to slather the toast in butter, then roll it up, eating it like a hot dog.

It's impossible to overstate how pleasurable this was for those who got their toast while it was still hot enough to melt the butter.

The rookies, of course, got only cold slices; but those who served the toast early and hot were at least spared the hazing and beating that befell those further back in the production line.

Δ

This whole toast thing was terribly sad. Even sadder was how much time I spent thinking about it back then. All of us did. On any given day, it was the only thing that really mattered.

10

You have to wonder sometimes about your delusions. Like the idea I had that only members of a highly select group—an elite—were accepted to the seminary. That being allowed to enter was tantamount to ordination. I entered with that notion even though I'd never heard of anyone who'd applied and been turned away. Nor had there ever seemed to be any suspense over whether I'd be accepted. Yet I persisted in this conviction that you had to be exceptionally intelligent and devout to get in.

Once inside, though, it was ridiculously clear that the only qualification for admission was asking to be admitted. And I was immediately able to put each of my fellow seminarians into one of four categories, all of them lowly: the retarded, the psychologically disturbed, the cruel, and the faux worldly. None fit any description I could conjure up of what a "potential priest" should be like.

Δ

That term "retarded"—I mean, in those days, it wasn't necessarily a pejorative term; it was just descriptive, clinical. The first such seminarian I noticed was an upperclassman—in his third year by then—whom everyone called "Sweet Pea." I don't remember ever learning his actual name. He was gangly, clumsy, with narrow sloping shoulders, a pointed head, pale blue eyes, extremely fair skin, and a haircut that left an incongruous gob of tight curls sticking straight up above his forehead. Everything about him broadcast his vulnerability.

His speech was halting and painfully slow. He never seemed quite able to understand anything, which made for no end of opportunities for hilarity. He had the face of a simpleton—open, dim, confused. I could never look at him without thinking of Lenny in *Of Mice and Men*.

Δ

We were playing an intramural baseball game one day when this other upperclassman, Mike Lincoln, was on the mound for one team, Sweet Pea playing for the other. Lincoln was mean. With Sweet Pea batting early in the game—and by "batting," I mean "standing in the batter's box to take his three strikes"—Lincoln looked in for the catcher's signal, then shouted, "Fastball? Fastball? You want me to throw a fastball?" Then he wound up and threw a curve right at Sweet Pea's head. Sweet Pea collapsed in a panicked heap, his bat flying, his limbs flailing, as the ball broke over the plate and the umpire dolefully called a strike.

No one laughed. Sweet Pea was retarded in a clinical sense that wasn't his fault—he wasn't like Richard/Reechard/Retard who, being socially retarded, was therefore a legitimate target for abuse—and we all understood that he was to be pitied rather than tormented. But no one rebuked Lincoln, either. And for some reason, he just looked kind of pissed instead of pleased with himself.

Maybe it was his way of feeling ashamed, I don't know. We all knew that Sweet Pea wasn't capable of hitting the ball, so the trick was all the more egregious for its being completely unnecessary from the baseball-strategic perspective. No sooner did Sweet Pea literally fall for it than everyone watching kind of sunk into collective shame. And Sweet Pea, in his simplicity, his innocence, just got up and stepped back into the batter's box.

Episodes like that—usually sans the shame—were part of the routine in the seminary, built into the schedule along with Matins, Lauds, Mass, classes, meals, work, Vespers, lights out. Every class singled out its weaklings for constant punishment, and every class was led by guys like Lincoln.

Δ

There were three designated victims in our class— Mike Rainier, another apparently retarded kid; Greg King, an earnest, anxiety-ridden nervous breakdown waiting to happen; and a hapless, highly rules-observant seminarian named Greg Foster, nick-named Fidel during his rookie year, who was just universally disliked for some reason I never figured out. They were singled out practically the day they arrived, and remained in their roles for all their years in the seminary.

Rainier was hopelessly slow-witted. His most memorable victim's moment came in typing class one day during our sophomore year. The typing lab had these big manual typewriters, which even then seemed antiquated. Some of the quicker wits in class loosened all the screws holding the platen in place on Rainier's typewriter, so that when he got to the end of the line he was laboriously typing and lustily pushed the carriage return lever, the platen went flying halfway across the room. Even Father Grabowski, a humorless little priest who was so socially crippled that he could be assigned nothing by way of ministry other than teaching seminary typing classes, couldn't help but smile.

Δ

For some reason, pranks pulled on Sweet Pea were sad, but pranks pulled on Rainier were funny. And they never left you with that creepy feeling you have when you've hurt a helpless person. This was most likely because Rainier never seemed hurt by any of these pranks. He genuinely seemed to believe, nearly every time, that some random accident had befallen him, and if he did understand that he was being played for a fool he would take it as a sign of affection. It never occurred to him that his fellow seminarians were capable of cruelty towards him. The weird aftermath of these incidents always left me looking at him in wonderment, and thinking he was destined for a seamlessly happy life. It was as if he enjoyed special protection, conferred by God—insulation from sorrow; I came to think of him as a Holy Fool.

Δ

It was different with King. He was the kind of thin that is caused by unrelenting anxiety—like he was perpetually on a psychological treadmill that had him shedding pounds faster than he could take in calories. He was the only student there who was as skinny as I was. You could count his ribs from across the dorm, and the vertebrae on the back of his neck, the scapulae, the clavicles—they all stood out with frightening prominence. He just flat-out exuded pathos, his eyes blinking madly, his lips contorting, his speech a stammering rush. He was always talking through his saliva, too, the combination of his voice's mushy sound with the rush of his words causing us to label him "Gosh Guyzh"—an invocation of his nerves, his drainage problem, his earnestness, and the way he began every statement.

He had this nervous-twitchy way of swaying from side to side when he walked or tried to run. Kneeling in prayer, his shoulders would be hunched up to his ears, his head bowed, his hands clenched in front of his face, his eyes squeezed shut. The rest of the time, his shoulders were perfectly straight, like he was constantly braced for an expected blow from above. His body just could not relax.

And after every single class, whatever the subject, he would walk up to the teacher to ask One More Question. Especially after religion class, which always seemed to have him tied up in knots.

There was only one class the whole time he was there after which he elected not to walk up to the teacher and ask a question. And that class was one that had us all scurrying out of the classroom with him as quickly as we could: Father Foster's lecture on sex.

11

I can't seem to make myself tell this story properly, no matter how much time I set aside for it each day. I sit down to write and my mind goes blank. What little I remember I remember out of order. Events this distant, this troubling…recollection of those days is like a guttering candle, little flickers of remembered episodes between vast black cold stretches—a little memory fighting to stay alight.

I waste my allotted writing time by tearing my house apart in search of distractions. It's not like ordinary writer's block, either—it's something more daunting, more telling.

I suppose it has to do with the nature of the memories. I mean, I'm not exactly trying to remember winning Wimbledon here; it was a grim time. And it's no fun remembering these characters—the Kings, the Rainiers, the Lincolns. Nor is it much fun remembering me.

Δ

I had exactly one hero that year: Cassius Clay. I kept the *Sports Illustrated* issue with him on the cover, posed in front of a pile of money said to be exactly $1 million, in my desk. I showed it to everyone who came near me, extolling his virtues, his brashness. Alone in study hall, I would take it out and stare at it, dreaming, wondering, venerating. I couldn't believe he was only seven years older than I was when he'd more or less conquered the world.

Δ

The thing about Greg King was, he never seemed able to develop any sense of caution. You could pull the same prank on him countless times, and each time it would look, from his reaction, to have been the first. Mark Moore, our class clown—he was nicknamed "Cub" because he bore a slight physical resemblance to Mark Reilly, from the class above us, who was nicknamed "Bear"—would contrive every day to be in the pew directly behind King at Mass. And every day, he would tie King's shoes together during the Consecration. And every time, King would rise to go take Communion and either stumble or fall outright. It just never, never, never occurred to him to check, or to detect Cub fooling around with his shoelaces. He was like Wile E. Coyote the way he gave the impression every single time that the prank had never been pulled on him before.

There were days when watching this little stunt unfold yet again made me feel like I was going completely insane.

Δ

Thus continued my inexorable (and now accelerated) slide from grace. My complicity, through silence, in the mistreatment of the afflicted. Sobering proof that I was no better than I'd been before I became a seminarian. Knowing full well that it was my Christian duty to intervene, I chose instead the path of weakness by saying nothing, and arguing to myself that it was enough not to join the torture sessions. Of course I knew that I was lying, committing a sin of omission, ignoring the admonition in Matthew, "Amen I say to you, as long as you did it to one of these my least brethren, you did it to me."

But then again, they literally *were* doing to it to me. Within weeks of my arrival, I had settled into the role of clown/victim, alternately getting laughs and getting pushed around. My confreres delighted in surrounding me—particularly in the dorm, when they could catch me shirtless—and pushing me back and forth inside their circle, calling me "Biceps," trying to get me to flex my meager muscles. And their mantra at most other times was the refrain, "Can you imagine Moody with a girl?" accompanied by a chorus of chortles.

It turned out to be easy to play to that comparatively gentle mockery, cite it in my little interior moral debates as evidence that I couldn't be complicit with the tormenters since I myself was one of the tormented.

Δ

But then again it also was the height of vanity—a grievous sin of pride—to think yourself a person of such importance that your intervention could make a difference to anyone, either by influencing the tormenter or easing the burden of the tormented. Only the deadliest of sinners, the most vain among us, could be capable of thinking himself a Savior.

Δ

It's a monstrous challenge, remembering anything from this remove—particularly since it involves a time in my life I've been determined to forget.

Δ

English I	A
Latin I	A
Algebra I	B
Anct. History	B
Sacred Doctrine I	A
Speech I	B

12

One of the first people there to really stand out to me as remarkable, thought-provoking, was a kid named Leon. He was an ex-seminarian, a member of the class ahead of mine, who had been kicked out at the end of his first year. He kept coming back all the time to visit. He'd show up in the evening, during free time, and people—his old classmates, curious rookies like me—would gather around to hear him tell stories about the outside. He always wore a black leather jacket, tight black jeans, had a ducktail haircut, and never failed to bring in cigarettes and alcohol. Which…I mean, I couldn't handle those things when I was fourteen: I tried smoking, which a ton of people in the seminary did all the time, but it just made me sick. And I was afraid of alcohol.

Leon exuded rebelliousness, derring-do, cool. He was glamorously pale—the antithesis of the surfer we all tried to emulate—and thin in a way that invited admiration rather than scorn. It made him look tough, that pallor. He carried a switchblade, which he was always bringing out, showing off how it worked. He would pass out cigarettes, light up, pass his bottle around, and regale us with stories of all the girls—Protestant girls!—he was making it with on the outside.

We loved hearing his stories, but at the same time there was something pathetic about him. It seemed to me that he was really dejected over having had to leave. You felt like he wished he could still be in the seminary, even though he went on and on all the time about how cool it was on the outside, and how much we were missing out on. And you had to wonder why he kept coming back, often on Friday nights when he should have been out having all those adventures he kept telling us about. He just had this big fat sad air about him, even though he was certifiably cool—it all deepened my conviction that life outside the seminary was basically terrifying.

13

Boys who aspired to religious life had two choices: to become either a Father or a Brother. To be a Redemptorist Father—a priest—required twelve years of education, six in the minor seminary, where I was now, and six in the major seminary in Oconomowoc, Wisconsin. To be a Brother was a simpler matter, requiring much less work and education. You couldn't perform sacraments—you were more less a workhorse for the Fathers—but you could lead a life of prayer, contemplation, sacrifice, and celibacy.

There was an elderly brother at the seminary named Brother Fred, who was never heard to utter a word. He was tall and gaunt, with a long face, square jaw, big thoughtful eyes. Contemplative, apparently simple. He did all the real work in the place—keeping machinery in working order, doing repairs to the buildings—and appearing always to be "at prayer," not only in chapel but wherever he was, whatever he was doing. He had a aura about him that came right out of the *Lives of the Saints*, and he was the only religious I ever encountered who made that impression on me—who seemed a Living Saint.

He was, in other words, the kind of man I'd expected everyone in a seminary to be: exuding religiosity, his life given over entirely to God.

Δ

From *The Coastline*, Spring 1963:

IN MEMORIAM
Larry Larson

Brother Fred was the tall lean man with the calloused hands who stretched them out with gentle grace.

I wondered how he could have any influence on my life. I never talked with him, but I knew he had a way of conversing that made you aware of the meaning of a "saint".

When I came to Holy Redeemer College in '61 my mind was filled with the excitement for the priesthood. The idea of going out and preaching and enriching souls with the knowledge of God by my words brought an overwhelming satisfaction of joy. I knew people were ignorant of sin and God and I wanted to capture every soul I came in contact with. I would have gone on every roof-top and sung my praise to God. Each time I went into Chapel, I looked up to the tabernacle and said, "Lord, You and I are going shoulder to shoulder to convert the world."

I know God wants everybody to be a saint, so I tried to fulfill His wish by my idea of a saint. I thought it was impossible—how could I calm myself down and kneel in chapel all day? But when I thought it over, I knew that this wasn't the way. I wanted the truth about sanctity. Here's where Brother Fred came in. I remember seeing him in chapel reading prayers or struggling through the Stations, with barely enough strength to move. I think I'll never forget that continuous cough he had, so deep and with a roughness that made me shiver. It seems that when he prayed he said every word with meaning—and then he made each prayer live in his daily life.

Everyday I saw him dressed with striped blue overalls slaving away in the workshop. He saw work was good, and when work was to be done he did it. He labored in silence so as to be completely conscious of his work, and of Him for whom he did it.

He was just another human, as you and I, with faults, sins and temptations. But he lowered his head in supplication—and God filled him with holiness.

You may think I'm being over-sentimental making good better than it really is. How can I look into his mind and see his thoughts? But a man's thoughts are revealed by what he does. And each time I go on a walk here at HRC I see Brother Fred's echo over and over again. He molded and shaped and formed HRC. And even further, look at the Redemptorists he helped along to their vocation! Look at the seminarians he has helped and is helping. His life was a continuous prayer to God for his fellow men. He now lies in peace with God. But he lives on in the memory of all who knew him.

Δ

My friend Mark Reilly and I were assigned the task of burning Brother Fred's things after he died. They brought the stuff out in boxes and stacked it in front of the incinerator—this big rusted metal stove in the turnaround outside the priests' and brothers' sleeping quarters. We started picking stuff up out of the boxes by the handful and throwing it into the fire.

Then one of the things I picked up turned out to be a whip.

It was a small leather item, with a six-inch-long handle and four or five strips of leather coming off it, with a hard knot on the end of each one.

It should have inspired awe, given all the reverence we had for the legendary saints of yore who spent their entire lives mortifying their flesh with hairshirts, whips, barbed wire, thorns, nails...this was a huge, overriding feature of Catholic mythology. But instead, this whip was like evidence of some terrible dark secret, like something a pervert does. It immediately gave Mark and me the creeps. We looked at each other, looked at the whip, felt this strange kind of terror come over us, and threw it in the fire as quickly as we could. And neither of us ever said a word to anyone else about it. For that matter, we never brought it up with each other again, either.

Δ

After he died, before his funeral, we had a twenty-four-hour vigil with Brother Fred's body, in chapel. Around the clock, a pair of us at a time, kneeling for an hour in cassocks on prie dieux at the foot of his open casket. My time, shared with King, was at three in the morning. King was nervous as hell—I think he was afraid Brother Fred was going to suddenly sit up in his casket or something— and all I could think about was that damned whip. I'd regard it alternately as evidence of some kind of secret evil or as proof positive of the absurdity of someone of my low moral status praying for the soul of a proven saint. As if my intercession was what it took for him to gain entrance into heaven.

Δ

Fred Moody

From *The Life of Saint Teresa of Avila by Herself*: "O God, in how many ways did Your Majesty set about preparing me for the state in which He wished me to serve Him! Thus, without my willing it, the Lord compelled me to do violence to myself. Blessed by He for ever! Amen."

Δ

Here was this inspiring Church tradition that had been drilled into us constantly since we first started Catholic school, physical self-torture being the most consistent feature running through Catholic history. We pretty much had no heroes other than martyrs and penitents. But when it came to the saintly living among us now, it was an entirely different matter, to judge from Mark's and my reaction to Brother Fred's Dark Secret of Sainthood. Why was something historically so inspiring coming across to us as creepy when discovered in someone living among us? What was so different about us—about our time—that made tangible evidence of sanctity something shameful?

Δ

I'm pretty sure that was the first time I'd had any intimation that there might be something fundamentally unhealthy about Catholicism: that what I'd taken for devotion to the one true religion might instead be some weird psychological illness.

14

Whenever we went on outings—we had these two decrepit buses we would ride when the whole seminary was taken out somewhere, like to Half Moon Bay or Yosemite…big deals, these kinds of trips—the upperclassmen at some point during the ride would lead the bus in this song, which was also a staple at parties we'd hold from time to time in the refectory:

Chorus:

Parties…make the world go round,

Parties…make the world go round,

Parties…make the world go round,

"Let's haaaave a party!"

Then the song leader would shout, "Girls in grass skirts!"

And everyone would shout, "Boooooo!"

Leader: "Guys with lawn mowers!"

Chorus: "Yaaaaay!"

Parties…make the world go round,

Parties…make the world go round,

Parties…make the world go round,

Fred Moody

"Let's haaaave a party!"

"Girls in tin skirts!"

"Boooooo!"

"Guys with can openers!"

"Yaaaaaay!"

And so on…they could go on for whole bus rides with this thing. There was always this strange lighthearted veneer over our life there, while underneath—at least for me—all was dark swirling confusion.

Δ

Which may have been brought on by what we had streaming in from the outside world. For all of our isolation, we somehow managed to be inundated along with the rest of the country by the Beatles and Bob Dylan. And there was something delightful, exciting, almost sinful in the way we would torment the seminary's surf-culture devotees with the news that their day was over, that the Beach Boys and Jan and Dean were going to be obliterated by the Beatles.

We had this tiny rec room in a little daylight basement of the classroom building, where we would gather around a little portable record player and play "Meet the Beatles" over and over again, all rec period long, day after day after day. We couldn't get enough of it—playing the album all the way through, Side 1 and Side 2, always in order, staring at the album cover, marveling at the outrageously long hair on the musicians. And—strangely—never feeling even the slightest twinge of guilt.

Next on line was the *Freewheelin' Bob Dylan* album—another mind-blower, particularly as its values were
so much in line with what we were being taught. Racial
equality, opposition to war.... We were awe-struck at the
poetic power of that album, and thoroughly taken with the
idea that someone out there who all but defined cool was
espousing (much more beautifully, powerfully) many of the
same teachings we were taking in from the Fathers.

I would find quiet times to sneak down to the rec
room with one or two friends—Dylan wasn't yet the sem-
inary-wide sensation the Beatles were—and listen to those
songs over and over again, staring at the album cover, marveling, reveling in this abiding connection with the outside.
I memorized pretty much all of the lyrics on the album and
could walk around all day singing, in my head, "A Hard
Rain's A-Gonna Fall." Stunning performances every time,
the voice in my head being very Dylanesque—raw, raging,
in tune, in marked contrast to my actual tone-deaf singing voice, which was as much a source of merriment to my
confreres as my biceps were.

I saw the Dylan of that album as a kind of fellow
seminarian, sacrificing everything for the sake of his stern
moral vision. Righteous. A preacher with real style—he
made our beliefs, our values, our principles, feel cool.

15

The most notable—and possibly the most scarring—event of that first year was our experience of the lecture given every winter to every rookie class by the seminary's spiritual director, Father Foster.

There were two priests who served as counselors, basically—chosen, from what I could tell, because of their ability to talk more or less normally with teenagers. Younger priests who came across as cooler, more relaxed, hipper than the regular Fathers.

Father Foster was this gruff-mannered priest who liked to hang out during work and recreation periods with the seminarians—playing basketball, shooting the shit, pitching in to help with work, helping coach sports teams. He was burly, swarthy, thickset, with a face permanently set in a friendly scowl.

We liked having him around during work and recreation periods—he was a funny guy. I remember one day working down on the ballfields with him—there were four or five us on that work crew—and when we stopped to watch one of the other seminarians ride a unicycle up the hill to the dorms, Father Foster said, "He looks like he's giving birth to a giraffe." It totally cracked us up.

Foster had this way of looking up at the ceiling or off to the side, tugging at his collar, and making little grunting noises when he was nervous or embarrassed about something. And was he ever embarrassed when he came in to give us The Lecture.

We were sitting in the classroom waiting for our Algebra teacher, Father Lester, to show up, when Foster walked in instead. Looking everywhere but at us. He stepped up on the platform at the front of the room, stared out the windows for a minute, then started talking.

Δ

Man, was he nervous. Completely different from how he normally was. Something was so clearly wrong that we all sat there scared at first, wondering if he was going to come down on us for something horrible somebody did. He hadn't been this opaque since the afternoon he popped his head into our classroom to announce that the president had been shot, and directed us to chapel to pray for him.

Whatever it was this time, it was clearly a big deal. Changes in seminary routine were unheard of. And he was acting really, really weird.

It didn't take long to figure out that the problem was even worse than we feared.

Δ

"Every year at this time we arrange for you freshmen to hear an important lecture—one that will supply you with the kind of knowledge that isn't covered in our normal curriculum but that nonetheless will prove very useful to you as priests. As parish priests or retreatmasters, you will be called on to deal with certain problems that married people will come to you about. Questions or problems will be brought to you that will be difficult for you to provide counsel on since your own vows will preclude you from having had certain opportunities to learn about them first-hand.

"So. There are certain basic things you have to understand if you are to be effective as priests, particularly those of you who will regularly counsel the laity. One of those things is human reproduction—which is what I've come here to discuss today."

Δ

Given that we had entered the seminary more or less to avoid everything having to do with this topic, the terror in the room positively soared. None of us now could look up at Foster…we just kept our heads down, staring at our desks.

Δ

"Well." Foster's voice was hurried, monotonous, like he was hoping he could speed time up by talking faster. "Let me begin by saying that sexual organs are good and beautiful—not disgusting or 'dirty' or in any way funny—because they are God-given for the noble purpose of continuing the human race, a creation of God. They should therefore be regarded with the reverence and respect we would accord any special gift of God."

He paused for a long time, then went into a more or less clinical recitation of the relevant body parts. After which he lapsed almost completely into the passive voice, with "eggs" being "fertilized" by "sperm" after the male "penis" is "placed" in the female "vagina." Not a lot of detail, and no intimation that people might do this for any reason other than to propagate, it being a mortal sin to engage in sexual intercourse when there was no possibility of impregnation—a point he…um…hammered home repeatedly.

Δ

The weird thing about this lecture was that we all knew there was something deeply wrong about it, that it was packed with misinformation. And this was a crowd that believed in—and could tell the difference between—the Virgin Birth and the Immaculate Conception.

Δ

"Then, if the egg is not fertilized by the end of the woman's monthly cycle, it and the nesting fluid are sloughed off, and passed through the vagina. This is called 'menstruation.' It generally lasts for about one week and is a very difficult time for the woman, who grows irritable and sometimes uncontrollably depressed. This depression is caused by the woman's natural longing for pregnancy, and since menstruation is a clear signal that she has failed to conceive, she is overcome with shame and disappointment—hence her depression. She should be treated with extra care and consideration during this time. Many of the marital problems that priests are called upon to resolve have their roots in this phenomenon."

Δ

The problem for women was that much as they yearned for pregnancy, they weren't so hot for sexual intercourse. "The nature of sexual pleasure is entirely different

Fred Moody

for the man than for the woman. A man's only real sexual pleasure is experienced during intercourse—the only part of his body that responds deeply to sexual stimulation is his penis, and his greatest pleasure is when his sperm is ejaculated. The pleasure a woman derives from the act of intercourse is different, and much more subtle. It consists of a mild sweat that breaks out over her entire body. For the woman, the greater pleasure comes from the comfort and feeling of protection she gets from her husband's affection. She is much more pleased by being held in her husband's arms than in taking part in the act of intercourse. 'This is warmth, this is security, this is what *I want!*' she is saying, while the husband is intent only on intercourse."

Δ

Did this ever make us feel creepy.

Δ

At the entrance to the seminary, where you came in from Golf Links Road, you could see to your right a new monastery under construction, where the Fathers were going to move. On the left was a cyclone fence, on the other side of which was someone's house. The people there had this big yard where they kept a peacock and peahen. That peacock was insanely loud—he would let off these shrieks that you could hear all over the seminary grounds—and he would spread this spectacular tail, a huge array of green-and-blue circles on this massive feathery fan. And he had an iridescent blue chest that he would puff out whenever he spread out that big tail of his. He was basically magnificent, and he knew it.

It seemed like whenever I looked over there, I'd see him with that tail spread, shrieking, while the lowly gray drab peahen was just kind of skulking around like the last thing she wanted was to be noticed by that guy.

Δ

Father Foster didn't really give us all that much time to sort out why we felt there was something wildly wrong with what he was telling us. It was weird—I mean, none of us had any basis from reading or experience or any other source of information for thinking that he was giving us misinformation, but we just *knew* that what he was telling us was wrong.

He kept plowing ahead. After a brief mention of the "point of no return"—the moment in which it is impossible to reverse course and prevent ejaculation, as he explained it, making it sound like a dramatic moral battle ending in ignominious defeat—he shifted from the mechanics of marriage to moral questions related to pleasure and will. "It is very important to note that even though the act of sexual intercourse is intensely pleasurable, it is a sin to indulge in it solely for the sake of pleasure. That is, there must be at least the possibility that pregnancy could result from the act of intercourse for it not to be sinful."

Δ

"Experiencing sexual pleasure—even ejaculation—outside of sexual intercourse is not in itself a sin, as sometimes such events happen involuntarily. There may be times—for instance, when one is bathing, or having a certain kind of dream—when sexual pleasure can arise unexpectedly, without your having desired it or willed it to happen, and under such circumstances the particular action itself would not be sinful so long as one does not intend the pleasure that results, and does not consent to it if it spontaneously arises. In such cases only an individual conscience can provide the answer. Just remember that your conscience can never be made to lie to you, and if you have even the slightest misgiving about one of these 'accidental' episodes you have more than likely committed a sin, and should go to confession."

Δ

There followed a fairly long disquisition on the difference between an "occasion of temptation" and an "occasion of sin." This afforded us considerable relief, as it moved us into more comfortably dispassionate Catholic territory, where the wrestling was more or less intellectual. "Let's say, for example, that you open a magazine without realizing what is inside it, and you come upon a picture that arouses you. You have entered an occasion of temptation—an unexpected source of temptation to sin. It is an occasion of temptation instead of an occasion of sin because you'd never encountered it before. As long as you cease the activity, close the magazine, put the picture out of your mind before voluntarily taking pleasure in it, you have committed no sin, for you never intended to submit yourself to temptation. If, however, you were to return to that magazine and reopen it knowing what you would find inside, you are then entering an occasion of sin rather than an occasion of temptation. The difference lies in the foreknowledge."

Δ

When the bell signaling the end of the class day went off, we cleared out of there in record time. All you could hear was the scraping of our chairs and the shuffling of our feet. It's the only class I remember when no one stayed behind to ask a question, no one talked on the way out of class, no one lingered waiting for one friend or another.

I can't speak for anyone else in attendance, but I left feeling kind of dirty. And I suppose it's telling that not one of us said a word to anyone else in the class about that experience. It was like we all secretly agreed to pretend that it hadn't ever happened.

Δ

The only thing that came close to matching this lecture for its combination of murkiness and the feelings of discomfiture it provoked was the running series of warnings we were given all year long about "particular friendships." The Fathers never actually defined this term; they simply warned us against these things, which we understood to be the cultivation of a friendship with one confrere that deliberately excluded everyone else. Whenever a Father uttered the term, it would just hang there in the air, giving us the sense that nothing on earth could be more menacing.

16

It wasn't all that long after Father Foster's lecture that we went on one of our daylong outings to a beach. This one was a trip to Half Moon Bay, a little more than an hour away on our buses—a solid hour of listening to "Parties Make the World Go 'Round."

Δ

We stepped off the bus into a glorious day at what up to that time was the most beautiful place I'd ever seen. Pure sand on the beach, as opposed to the rocks and pebbles that covered the Puget Sound beaches where I grew up; massive surf, huge cliffs, swirling mist with bright blue skies overhead, perfect comforting warmth—I was plunked down in the middle of yet another absolute fantasy of California.

I started walking up the beach—since I couldn't swim, I was afraid to go near the water—with various small groups of seminarians ahead of me. After I'd walked a couple hundred yards, I saw everyone up ahead lying prone and peering over a ridge of sand, laughing, pointing, gesturing to those of us behind to hurry up and come see what was happening. They were insane from the excitement—that much I could tell even from a distance.

When I got up there, they were whooping, pointing, laughing in utter disbelief—most of them were, at any rate. King and a couple others had turned their backs on the show and looked really mortified.

Δ

I looked where they were pointing and saw a blanket covering a humped shape that was moving up and down rhythmically, rapidly. Naturally, I had no idea what I was looking at. It took a minute or more for the realization to dawn on me, and with it complete confusion.

I had had no idea, for one thing, that "placement of the penis in the vagina" so that "sperm" could be "deposited" there, involved so much frantic motion. I'd assumed the couple just lay there while the transfer took place on its own.

Instead, "sexual intercourse" apparently was a wild and violent transaction, involving no end of bucking and pumping. I was thoroughly confused and at the same time frantically trying to hide my confusion from everyone else, out of embarrassment. It was clear that I knew less about this business than everyone else in the seminary.

Finally the action stopped, and we watched the girl crawl out from under the quilt a few minutes later. We—all of us—had been waiting breathlessly to see what she looked like.

She was a teenager, no older than we were. And of course she was beautiful—how else to explain the guy's frenzy? And I was sure, even from a distance, that she looked terribly sad. She stood there looking out over the ocean and closed the zipper on the hip of her pedal pushers. The guy under the blanket was lying there so still you'd have thought he'd died.

17

It may have been coincidence, I don't know, but within a few days of that lecture and that trip, this classmate of mine, Jim Winfrey, commenced a series of performance pranks that would continue for the next three years.

Winfrey was a dedicated weirdo. His chief delight in life came from making people feel uncomfortable. He had a pigeontoed walk and a head shaped like a gigantic peanut M&M. His face was vivid: Paul Newman blue eyes and skin that he could turn a deep, aggressive, red shade at will. It was like it was controlled by a switch, that face of his, the way it would light up. Plus his voice was low, kind of metallic, and without any breathiness to it. Very eerie and resonant. He would go into these apparent trances where he would lower it even further and talk in a robotic monotone that gave you the creeps. You'd try to engage him, talk to him, distract him, somehow make him stop, but he wouldn't appear to be hearing you. It was weirdly compelling—you just couldn't stop watching once he set off on one of those riffs of his.

This new thing he started…I mean, he would just zero in on someone—usually someone like King or Rainier—and fix his creepy eyes on them, go into his trance, and intone, "Control your body." Over and over again, "Control your body. Control. Your. Body." There was something so hypnotic about it that everyone within earshot would sit there waiting for something supernatural to happen, and the target of his rebuke would grow more and more uncomfortable the longer Winfrey kept staring and intoning at him. It was hilarious, but it also secretly scared the hell out of people, the way he gave you the impression that he could see into your soul, to where your darkest secrets were stored, make you feel that you more than anyone else on earth had a desperate need to "control your body."

Δ

Also around that time, I noticed how certain students would start being singled out because they were pretty. They'd usually be smaller than everybody else, with blond hair and fair skin, and just generally...pretty. Bigger seminarians were always pawing them, grabbing them. Like this one classmate, Don Kalvin, the Baby Huey guy, who was the most aggressive offender—he would wrap a big meaty arm around one of these helpless little seminarians, hug him tightly to his chest, then stroke his hair and cheek over and over again, saying in this soft, dreamy voice, "So soft and fine...so soft and fine...."

Other kids who were deemed effeminate in one way or another but who weren't as pretty—they were just called "fems." Their treatment was different, in that it had an element of derision lacking in the treatment accorded the really pretty seminarians.

Δ

It was a little hard not to feel uncomfortable about all this at the time, but it was just another of those many disquieting feelings you'd get without really understanding why. Which was pretty much a staple of that whole first year in the seminary, that unease.

Δ

We were all excessively modest, afraid ever to let anyone else ever see our bodies—particularly those good and beautiful things of ours. We wore bathrobes when going back and forth between our beds and the jakes. We showered in individual stalls, careful not to disrobe until the shower door was closed and secured. Our lockers, which ran along the walls of the dorm, were big wooden compartments that we would all but climb into to dress or change clothes. You would open your locker door, then stand facing into the locker to change, always keeping your bathrobe on until you'd safely gotten your trousers on. King of course was the most intent on modesty, even finding a way to get in and out of his shirts while keeping his robe on—an exercise we all loved to watch.

It was funny, though, how no one ever teased him about it; it was the only thing in his life there that he didn't get mercilessly razzed about.

18

It seemed like everything that happened at Holy Redeemer—particularly anything involving fun or pleasure— eventually sent you into fear-soaked ruminations about sin. It was impossible—for me, at any rate—to take uncomplicated pleasure in anything.

If it feels good, rue it.

That sense of sinfulness lurked beneath everything, every special occasion. Even in chapel, where your mind would wander from prayer and meditation into territory where, even if the subject matter itself wasn't sinful, the act of wandering, of giving in to the urge to be distracted, was.

Δ

But then again we were always undercutting the seriousness with which I had expected us to be living as we guided our lives toward our vocations. It was impossible to be properly contemplative as per my various hopes and dreams when certain wags would constantly delight, for example, in breaking Silence with a fart, after which people around the offender would lick the air…a relatively regular occurrence. And then during recreation periods you'd have someone starting up a mock-serious debate on whether farting during Silence was a sin, in that one would be "breaking the Silence," possibly on purpose, etc. etc. etc. That was about as profound as spontaneous theological debates ever got in that place.

Δ

AN INSIDE STORY
Greg Foster

"What's it like to be a seminarian?"

Many times I have been asked that question, and it's not an easy one to answer. I usually wind up answering, "Well, you just have to be one to see for yourself." I will say this, though, it is a beautiful life, a life that satisfies every desire.

When I arrived at Holy Redeemer College it was a cheerful, sunny day. I will never forget that day for a long time. I was now, officially, a seminarian. A new seminarian is usually very impressed with HRC, not so much the place, but rather the guys. After five minutes, I was no longer a stranger. The older men made me feel like a genuine rookie, which indeed I was, and would be for the entire year. It was a good feeling, but more important, I was now so close to Our Lord, so easily! Everything in life now had so much more meaning and purpose.

As time goes on, you can't help but grow in love for God, and for the vocation that you have chosen. And because of all this I realize, now, why I am a seminarian, and what I must do. And, as a seminarian, I am fast approaching my goal, the priesthood – That goal which is now so precious and so dear to me. As a seminarian, I live a happy life full of many joys. I am really happier than I have ever been. But, as I have so often said, "You just have to be one to see for yourself."

19

The seminary grounds were pretty huge. They occupied this valley where you would enter through a gate off Golf Links Road on the east end of the property, at more or less the highest point, then go by the Fathers' new living quarters on the right, then a tennis court/basketball court on the left, then cross a little bridge over a creek, pass through the main complex of buildings, then go down a pretty steep hill to the playfields below. The road leveled off there and ended way down at the foot of the playfields, at a locked gate that opened out into a rough Oakland neighborhood.

Right where the hill flattened out, there were ballfields on the right. On the left, up against a steep hill covered with poison oak, was our auditorium. This was the place where we would go once a month for movies, Movie Night being a really big deal. For some reason, we were able to get movies that were pretty new, so it wasn't like we were watching some dorky old movie that normal people weren't interested in anymore.

Like the only movie I remember from our freshman year: *The Cardinal*, starring Tom Tryon, who was a big star at the time. *Texas John Slaughter* had been one of my favorite TV shows growing up, and for people like me it was a big thrill to have this cool handsome star (so cool he could make a Yosemite Sam-style hat look cool) play a Catholic figure—in this case, a cardinal.

When the movie starts, Tom Tryon is being promoted or elevated or whatever to Cardinal—he's in the middle of the ceremony when he flashes back to his ordination, and the whole movie until the end is him remembering his life as a series of Catholic clichés punctuated by moral crises. Even then, and even though we all sat through all three hours of this movie in rapt silence, most of it was silly: his big Boston Irish Catholic family, the various stock characters (curmudgeonly monsignor; saintly pastor in a poverty-stricken parish; gorgeous young woman who assists said saint by cooking his meals, caring for him while he's sick, etc., before she enters a convent; Ku Klux Klansmen with gross redneck accents; various crisp Nazis during the rise of Hitler…the guy really got around on his way to making it to cardinal).

Δ

The part of the movie that shook me—and like everything that troubled me in those days, I was afraid to talk about it out loud with anyone—had to do with Tom Tryon's sister. When he visits home after being ordained, there are indications that she's a tad wild—going out at night, coming home late, arguing with her virtuous sister, etc. etc. etc. When he comes home to visit after being assigned to a nearby parish, she tells him she's in love…but with a Jew. The relationship founders over the Catholic teaching at the time mandating that a non-Catholic must convert to Catholicism in order to marry a Catholic or must at least agree to raise the children as Catholic. The fiancé gives it a try, going to classes on Catholicism, but ultimately refuses to do either.

There follows a dramatic scene in which Tom Tryon's sister goes to Confession, with Tom Tryon as the confessor, and confesses that she slept with her ex- fiancé in the hope that he would change his mind. Tom Tryon is stern, nearly furious, clearly shocked, telling her that in order to be forgiven, she would have to give him up forever. Plus she would have to say ten rosaries—a very stiff penance by the Confession standards of those days. She storms out of the confessional and disappears, to be found a few months later living a life of sin as a risqué Tango dancer who stares defiantly at her brothers in the audience while publicly sinning on the dance floor.

Δ

Years pass; the sister is found in a flophouse, pregnant, in labor, screaming. Tom Tryon, with one of his brothers and her ex-fiancé, gets her to a hospital. A doctor comes out to tell the three of them that the sister's "birth canal" is "abnormally small" and that the baby's head is "abnormally large." The only way to save the mother is to crush the baby's skull. While Tom Tryon's brother and the ex-fiancé look on in horror, Tom Tryon says that the death of his sister would be "God's will," whereas intentionally killing the baby would be "murder." So he tells the doctor to let the mother die if that is the result of letting the baby live. There is a brief objection from the ex-fiancé, who now wants his girlfriend back and is willing to convert, etc. etc. etc., but the doctor explains that only the "next of kin" can make this decision, and the scene ends abruptly with the doctor going off to help with the fatal delivery.

Δ

Fred Moody

The next memorable scene is of a birthday party at Tom Tryon's family's home, celebrating the third birthday or so of an adorable little red-headed girl. And a few scenes/years later, Tom Tryon returns to Boston from Rome, to visit his family again, and is greeted at the airport by his beautiful teenaged niece, the message about God's will coming through loud and clear—particularly since the beautiful niece is virtuous, wholesome, and devout. But just in case you don't get it, Tom Tryon's mother says something to him about "God's will," while gazing adoringly at her dead bad daughter's living good daughter.

Δ

I just could not get this part of the movie out of my mind. And still can't. It has come back to memory over and over again over all these years. I suppose it's because it does capture—perfectly, sadly—the Catholic Church of that day, in all its smugness and rigidity, two years or so before the invention of the birth control pill (invented, for the record, by a Catholic). But something about the choice Tom Tryon is forced to make felt ridiculously false at the time. I tied myself up in knots trying to figure out what was wrong with it, but I couldn't fight my way out of the box the movie puts you in.

Still, that conviction that I was being deceived, cheated—even without knowing there was such a thing as a Caesarian section—just would not go away. I sat there during the movie trying to argue against it, but couldn't get anywhere—I just didn't know enough about what I was seeing to see the lie in it. All I knew was that I was terribly troubled by what felt like cheap manipulation.

But the most troubling thing about this little secret crisis of mine was that I understood that I was fighting not against the movie and its tricks but against Catholicism itself. That's where I felt the manipulation, the lying, was coming from.

20

There were certain things you could count on seeing every day during that first year. Big Don Kalvin wrapping his meaty arm around little blond Tom Roland, crushing him against his chest, stroking his hair and cheek repeatedly, saying over and over again, "So soft and fine...." Winfrey going into his "Control Your Body" trance. Fr. Lester answering an Algebra question from a hopelessly confused student with "Just keep your wits about you." Someone snapping his towel at King on the way to the jakes in the morning, and no one intervening to defend him; King walking up to the teacher at the end of every class and saying, "Say, Father, I was wondering...." The fury that would well up in you when you could see so clearly that King was offering up his suffering to God—that amazing patience so admirable in the *Lives of the Saints* was just infuriating when seen up close like that.

Δ

And every night after dinner that spring, walking with Bob Dolan up and down the road that ran from our buildings down past the auditorium to the gate at the foot of the property. It was an established tradition at the seminary, the walk up and down that road after dinner and before evening study hall. There'd be countless groups of two or three traversing the hill. We would always walk in the same groups, every night, with my group being me and Bob, or me and Bob and Greg McLeod. Every night, without fail, for nearly two years.

Δ

It seemed really sudden, the end of that rookie year. I remember coming back to the dorm after study hall maybe two nights before we had to leave for the summer and realizing that I had to leave, and that I was dreading the trip home. I'd gone home for Christmas six months before, but had hardly given home a moment's thought since. And even at Christmas, after only four months in the seminary, I had been anxious to get back. Somehow, somewhere along the line, the seminary had become "home"—where I'd grown up was the lesser place now.

We talked about it, my confreres and I, all of us coming to the same realization. And all of us thinking it was weird. How our goodbyes to each other were a lot more emotional than our goodbyes from our former homes had ever been.

I reminded myself to be sure to get a haircut next day, before leaving. I hadn't let anyone cut my hair since Christmas, as I'd been trying to grow it out so I could have big cool bangs like surfers had.

Δ

The problem was that my hair was too thick and curly—it just grew straight out and would never flop down over my eyes. I kept thinking if I grew it long enough it would finally flop over and give me proper bangs that I'd be able to fling extravagantly off my forehead with that little nonchalant surfer head-toss everybody else could pull off. I kept brushing and brushing this huge thick hairball that grew out on my head, trying to get it to behave, but it was hopeless.

Fred Moody

But getting it cut—that was such an obvious gesture, such an unignorable sign that I was going home to a much more restricted life, false to what I really was now. After a year in the seminary I was less devout, less religious, less subservient than I'd ever been back home. Now I felt that I'd grown into a different person and was being forced to regress. So I was going home a liar—not just because of the haircut, but because of all the things I knew now, had become now, that I could never dare reveal to the folks.

Δ

EDITORIAL

The prop-jet was ready for its flight to Reno, Nevada, where it would take its passengers for a weekend of relaxation. Eighty passengers were aboard – There was room for one more.

A couple all set for their vacation, stood by the gate waiting to board. Then came the bad news – There was only one seat left, so they had the choice of either splitting up, leaving one at the airport, as the other took the long awaited vacation – Or they could both stay home, cancelling all that they had planned. Not being contented with either of the alternatives, they tried desperately to arrange for two seats, they talked, and argued, as the plane shot exhaust over the runway. A man behind the couple, who also wanted to take this flight, pushed his way up to the gate where he bellowed out, "I'll take that seat." In minutes he was into the plane, up into the air, leaving the couple stranded, and disappointed. But soon their disappointment was changed, as the news spread across the nation, the plane had crashed, all on board were killed.

A man in a hurry – A man that had lost his patience, and his life. A selfish man who thought more of himself, than he did for others.

Many times we too become victims of these small failings – But we laugh when we think of them taking our lives. But chances are that if you would have told the man at the airport that they would take his, he would have laughed too.

Mike Fisher

Δ

English I	A
Latin I	A
Algebra 1	B
Anct. History	A
Sacred Doctrine I	B
Speech I	A

Δ

REMINDERS FOR SUMMER VACATION

Attend Mass faithfully and be on time every SUNDAY and HOLYDAY.

Feast of the Assumption of the Blessed Virgin Mary......August 15.

Go to Mass and receive Holy Communion on First Friday in honor of the Sacred Heart. We know you won't forget the First Saturday in honor of the Immaculate Heart of Mary.

First Fridays	First Saturdays
June 7	June 1
July 5	July 6
August 2	August 3

Say your morning and night prayers, and be faithful in saying the family Rosary, even if you only say it with one member of your family.

Go to Confession every week or two weeks and receive Holy Communion as often as possible.

Read at least 10 books during vacation.

Watch your citizenship grow by doing two extra good works each day.

21

During my first year, my dad and a friend of his had started a side business—a little downtown store called "Lakeway Card and Gift Shop." They sold Catholic products—rosaries, pictures of the Last Supper, saints' medals—along with standard secular card-shop stuff. My dad put me to work there, eight hours a day, paying me half the minimum wage. He got around the minimum-wage law by paying me $1.25 per hour, every other hour. I'm still not sure how that worked, legally speaking—but in any event, it didn't really matter since I turned all my earnings over to him anyway, to help pay for the seminary.

Δ

Everyone I had left behind when I entered the seminary seemed so dramatically changed that there was no longer any way for us to communicate. My neighbor, Rick Bergholz, a Protestant, with whom I'd run around pretty much every summer day when we were growing up, was all but unrecognizable. A year older than I, he had a driver's license and his dad had gotten him a car—a Volkswagen beetle. We took off in it one day—the only time I was to see him that summer. He was really proud to be driving. Shifting gears at one point, he looked over to me and said, leering, "This shift gets in the way of the ol' love muscle." Embarrassed, I thought it best after that to stay away from him—and from all my other worldly friends.

Δ

It made for a painfully slow summer. Work, church, yardwork at home, hiding out in my room, sitting on the living room couch staring out our picture window at the street. Meals in near-silence—I felt weirdly estranged from everyone, even my siblings.

There were Saturdays when I walked down to our church, half a mile away, and sat inside just for something to do, somewhere to hide.

Δ

I always entered and left our house through the back door. I would go down the four steps from our tiny back porch, walk through the fenced back yard to a gate beside the garage, and come out on the alley that ran the length of our block. From there, I would either walk through the yard of the neighbor across the alley, ending up in Broadway Park on the next block, or I would turn left and go up to Cornwall Avenue, the main street through our neighborhood and the street that led to church and on to downtown Bellingham beyond.

The Rinkers—a Protestant family with five girls— lived in the house on Cornwall next to the alley. They had a basketball hoop hanging over their garage door; everybody in the neighborhood gathered there to play basketball on summer nights.

The Rinker girl who was my age—Bev—was California gorgeous: blonde hair, blue eyes, and somehow always tan—quite a feat in our part of the country. Before I'd entered the seminary, she was part of the crowd of neighborhood boys and girls always playing basketball at her place. Now, like her older sister, she'd more or less stopped playing with the boys. The summer before I'd left, we had an awkward moment or two positioning for rebounds, grabbing at the ball together, locking eyes…mortifying, frightening, exciting, embarrassing for me.

And now I noticed when I saw her for the first and only time that first summer after coming home that she was wearing a little silver football suspended from a necklace—a sign that she was going steady with someone. I felt this absurd little twinge of devastation.

We chatted awkwardly for a while before she took an uncharacteristic turn for the serious. "So…if you're going to become a Catholic priest, that means you give up girls forever, right?"

"Yeah."

"I just don't see how you can make a decision like that when you're so young." And she stood there batting her eyes, coquettishly. As if she took my decision as a challenge.

"It's not that simple," I imagined myself replying. "It was either enter the seminary or constantly make a fool of myself in front of you, because of you."

Δ

I used to hate it when things like that popped into my mind without warning. I knew that it was the Truth breaking through, trying to get me to face reality. I'd beat myself up with the accusations that these unpremeditated thoughts had to be telling me what I really felt—in which case my being in the seminary was a lie, a sin.

22

On the train ride back to the seminary at the end
of summer, I noticed me and quite a few of my confreres
referring to Holy Redeemer as "home," as in, "It's nice
to be finally going home." It felt a little weird…isolating.
Like our life in the seminary was an ever-deepening secret,
something impossible to talk about with anyone on the outside.

Δ

BACKYARD VIEW
By Greg Vernon

The day in Oakland had turned out to be sunny and
warm. We had begun to feel the day's heat when we finally
boarded the bus that would take us within six or seven
blocks of the college. I casually glanced at my watch. It was
a quarter past five. The day had begun at nine thirty that
morning when we piled off the train. From there we split
up into groups of five or six. With two or three second year
men leading each group we had spent an enjoyable day in
Oakland. We went bowling; had lunch and took in a movie.
Now we were on our way to what we had come for, Holy
Redeemer College.

As the bus struggled through the rush-hour traffic I
took a quick and final glance at the city. It was a quarter to
six when we jumped off the bus. Deciding that it would be
good to have dinner at the corner hamburger stand we ordered a meal of burgers, shakes, root beer and French fries.

Time began to move faster and the burgers weren't cooking any quicker. By the time everyone paid his bill it was five to six. We were supposed to check in at six. It was a long six blocks, all uphill, to the college.

Our fast walk turned into a dash as the minute hand neared twelve. One of the veterans (a second year man) remembered a certain hole in the fence that would save some time. A little further, there was the hole and we were through it. My first sight, though it was a backyard view, had lived up to all my dreams. On the crest of a hill there were the classrooms and dormitory. The spire of the chapel overshadowed everything. Below was the ball field with its well-manicured infield. My stares were interrupted as one of the fellows yelled, "Come on!" "Hurry up!" The Angelus was sounding. Filing into the hall to say the Angelus I became a seminarian, God willing, until I am ordained.

Δ

We were considerably shocked when we walked through the gates and saw that the grounds had gone untended all summer long. All the grass was dead and everything was covered with knee-high brown weeds. The place looked like it had been abandoned for years.

And that evening, everyone was talking about Jim Winfrey's outburst when he came through the gate: "Fuck a duck! What have they done to this place?"

Δ

EDITORIAL
By Tom Harney

Father Rector welcomed us back to HRC with words of hope, both in the building project and in us, the students.

The steam shovels and cement trucks on the property prove that our dreams of an expanded college are now more than an enjoyable pastime. Everyday and every bucket of earth focus our goal more vividly.

But we must remember that new buildings and acres of property cannot make a happy community. We must mold in ourselves the Redemptorist spirit of giving. If we give enough, this year can be the best in HRC history. We have only to look at the faculty. The professors are giving their classes those extra sparks of dedication. They are all eager to give us their time and talents, the Science Club, the Art Club, the Student Choir.

But these men are only stairs. We must do the climbing.

Δ

The Angel of the Lord declared to Mary: And she conceived of the Holy Spirit.

Hail Mary, full of grace, the Lord is with thee; blessed art thou among women and blessed is the fruit of thy womb, Jesus. Holy Mary, Mother of God, pray for us sinners, now and at the hour of our death. Amen.

Behold the handmaid of the Lord: Be it done unto me according to Thy word.

Hail Mary, full of grace, the Lord is with thee; blessed art thou among women and blessed is the fruit of thy womb, Jesus. Holy Mary, Mother of God, pray for us sinners, now and at the hour of our death. Amen.

And the Word was made Flesh: And dwelt among us.

Hail Mary, full of grace, the Lord is with thee; blessed art thou among women and blessed is the fruit of thy womb, Jesus. Holy Mary, Mother of God, pray for us sinners, now and at the hour of our death. Amen.

Pray for us, O Holy Mother of God, that we may be made worthy of the promises of Christ.   Let us pray:

Pour forth, we beseech Thee, O Lord, Thy grace into our hearts; that we, to whom the incarnation of Christ, Thy Son, was made known by the message of an angel, may by His Passion and Cross be brought to the glory of His Resurrection, through the same Christ Our Lord. Amen.

Fred Moody

23

We spent the first two days out on grounds crew, mowing, watering, weeding, smoothing out the baseball diamond. Between the watering and the onset of California's autumn rainfall (gentle, warm, sweet…nothing like the perpetual cold downpour in the Northwest), the seminary was back to its glorious self within a week.

Δ

The new rookie class was smaller than ours had been—a sign of things to come. And our class wasn't into any of the traditional hazing that had always held sway at the seminary. We seemed that way about all the seminary traditions—we never took part in the "Parties Make the World Go 'Round" singalongs, for one thing—which seemed juvenile, embarrassing, un-hip. We seemed much more aware of, invested in, what was going on in the outside world than previous classes had been.

Δ

There was a profound difference from the previous year's arrival. I attributed it to my no longer being a newcomer—I was coming home now rather than going off into an unknown, and I was excited rather than scared. But it seems to me now there was something else in the air as well: a sense that great tumult was on the horizon. Huge changes in what we thought, believed, were coming. There's a line near the end of Dylan's *Chronicles: Volume 1*, as he discusses leaving the folk-music world in the mid-sixties: "In a few years' time a shit storm would be unleashed." You could feel it at the time, even in our cozy little retreat: the collapse of protective walls, the catastrophic opening of minds.

Δ

My interest in doing well in classes faded—particularly in Latin, which started revealing itself to be festering with indecipherable rules. The notion that I would become fluent in a dead language to the point where I would read, write, speak and think in it seemed laughable. And suddenly pointless. I would sit in my booth in language lab and distract myself from boredom by pulling little wads of the soundproofing out through the little holes in the panels on either side of me. You could sort of get purchase on it with the tip of your pen, and tease enough of it out to get a grip on it, then pull out a reasonably satisfying piece.

I already knew the Latin Mass and didn't see the point of trying to learn anything more than that, and Father Simpson, our Latin teacher, didn't seem all that interested in whether I was paying attention.

Δ

It wasn't boredom that dissuaded me from my studies so much as a dim sense that the goal—the priesthood— was no longer the main reason I was in the seminary. I didn't articulate it that way at the time; it was more that I just started drifting mentally, spiritually, psychologically, elsewhere.

Δ

My teachers were surprisingly indulgent. I was

never disciplined, never called back to attention in class. Not once did any of the Fathers complain about my disengagement, my wisecracking in class—now raised to an art form—my increasingly obvious disdain for their teaching. Only once, when Father Flodin—another of those socially inept Fathers who seemed shut off in the seminary mostly for their own protection—stopped lecturing long enough to come stand at my desk, did I realize that the Fathers actually did take note.

Father Flodin stood over me for a moment, staring down at me. I waited for the outburst, the punishment. But instead he gently patted me on the head and said, "Fred... poor Fred...you have the juices of life flowing through you right now...," at which point I was too distracted by the snickering of my classmates to hear the rest.

Δ

Of course I ridiculed Father Flodin, ridiculed his weird phrase, reveled in the celebrity the episode brought me. But I also secretly knew that he was on to something. I felt so jittery all the time that I could have sworn I saw little lightning bolts shooting out from my fingertips. And I could not stop talking, talking, talking. Silence was Hell that year—pure torture.

Δ

And it was as if Jim Winfrey's ongoing campaign was directed solely at me. I would walk into class to see a gigantic "CYB" written in letters that extended from top to bottom of the blackboard, with tiny squiggles trailing each letter. You had to all but press your nose to the blackboard to make out the little squiggles, which turned out to be written with astonishing clarity: "ontrol," "our," "ody."

"Control Your Body" was written everywhere: on blackboards, pavement, walls, in notes left in my locker.... And Winfrey would fix that mesmerizing stare at me, at me alone, and intone in that spine-tingling voice, "Control. Your. Body."

24

Aided and abetted by the Fathers, Dylan's *The Times They Are A-Changing* album more or less took over our lives. Our English and Religion teachers taught from it, Sunday sermons drew from its songs, particularly "Only a Pawn in Their Game" and "The Lonesome Death of Hattie Carroll"—and a group of us listened to it incessantly. It guided us morally and politically more than anything else in our lives that year, including our other religious teachings, and heightened our awareness of the political rumbling—the Free Speech movement in Berkeley, the United Farm Workers movement in California—starting to sound all around us. Our least brethren rising up. And it lent considerably to our understanding and sympathy for Cassius Clay in his conversion to Islam and change of name to Muhammad Ali.

Δ

But I can't think for you
You'll have to decide
Whether Judas Iscariot
Had God on his side

Δ

That year, the Fathers let us leave the grounds on weekends to take part in UFW demonstrations. We would hitchhike all over the Bay area to these events, carrying homemade signs—another in the long list of secrets I kept from my parents.

25

I decided to ignore the warnings from the Fathers about particular friendships. They were too undefined to seem legitimately dangerous—none of the Fathers ever told us what exactly made a friendship "particular." We were apparently just supposed to know one when we saw one.

I settled on the rationalization that the line between close friendship and particular friendship was so vague as to be meaningless—a stance brought on largely by my friendship with Bob Dolan.

We became inseparable. We sat at the same table at mealtimes, had adjacent desks in our classroom/study hall, hung out together between classes, were teammates in intramural football, baseball, basketball and soccer, and stayed together on outings, generally taking off on our own when we got to a destination. He wasn't my only close friend, but he was definitely the closest. I couldn't imagine giving any of that up—the sheer quiet sustaining joy of being around him—so I decided that whatever kind of friendship this was, it couldn't possibly be "particular." It felt too much like a blessing to be sinful.

Δ

My most troubling distraction that second year came by way of the kindness extended me by my classmate Denny Gonzales and his family. There were a few Sundays per year when families of seminarians were invited onto the grounds to attend Mass and spend the better part of the day visiting with their seminarian sons. They would bring picnic lunches, and most families would allow their sons to bring along a friend whose own family lived too far away to visit.

Denny and I had became fast friends—he was a generous-spirited soul who could see the good in everyone. Charitable in the most Christian sense of the word, and completely guileless and sincere about it. Not once in our three years there did I ever hear him say an unkind word about anyone. He exuded this kind of impossible aura— Catholic cool. It's hard to explain it other than to say that all these traits that came across in other people as contrived or dorky or mockable (as in the case of King and countless others) came across in Denny as something to be admired and emulated. He made virtue look as exciting and enviable as Leon did vice.

He had this added fascination for me in that he was Mexican American—the first nonwhite person I'd ever talked to, let alone befriended.

By the middle of my second year, his family had more or less adopted me. I'd go with Denny to their home on days we were allowed to leave the grounds, and they included me in every one of their visits. Every encounter, whether at their home or at the seminary, was augmented with amazing food. I couldn't get enough of this stuff, all of it unfamiliar, exotic. I was particularly taken with how every meal included tortillas, which I'd never seen before, and Coke, which I'd never been allowed to drink with meals.

It was sinful, of course, but for once I didn't care. Possibly because I had more grievous Gonzales-connected sins to contend with.

Δ

It wasn't just those meals with Denny's family. I was dealing constantly that year with the sensual. I couldn't turn my attention to anything without reacting with involuntary physical pleasure. My body seemed to have a will of its own—I was caught again and again and again by surprising, unexpected, sudden surges of pleasure. I'd turned from a contemplative aspiring priest into a mindless sense organ. Even listening to music—Dylan, the Beatles, Joan Baez— was no longer a simple intellectual or emotional exercise. Instead, I voluptuated in it—in the sound. It was as if I was listening with my body rather than my mind, feeling the music rather than hearing it.

Δ

And then one day Bob Dolan and I were down working on the ballfields when he paused to take off his shirt. He had his back to me; his skin was cream-smooth, his muscles rolling luxuriously underneath it …absolutely enchanting. I stared at him for a second with this sudden raging lust that I immediately suppressed with shame and terror.

Δ

EDITORIAL
By Pat Jacobson

I was once asked by a person, whom I later realized lacked a certain degree of faith, "…how can you stand to live in the same place, with the same faces and with the same old routine day after day, months on end?" Out of all the replies I could have given why I was dedicating myself to Christ I found myself saying, "for the same reason that you and every person living does anything—for happiness." We here believe our happiness and the salvation of our souls will be found in and on our way to our consecration to God as members of the great team, the Redemptorists. It is "In that same place" that we find a rich, rewarding valley where we can build our castles to our Creator. It is in these "same faces" that we see reflections of our own desires.

Whether we pray, play ball, study or work, with a single ideal we advance a little closer to our final goal—the priesthood. And it is in "the same old routine, day after day" that we find our building blocks to make our finished castles strong and enduring tributes to the Almighty Endower.

In this yielding we have indeed found a happiness. And we feel that we have something to be proud of. It is by the publication of this paper that we sincerely hope to share a little of our blessed happiness with you.

Δ

Whatever. Any time I wasn't spending with Bob Dolan I spent in tortured fantasy over Denny Gonzales' sister Rosa. I think she was a year younger than we were... I have no way of knowing, since I never had the nerve to ask Denny any questions about her, or to talk directly to her, or even to look her way unless I thought no one was looking. I can't even remember when I first noticed her— I just suddenly was obsessed, troubled, thrilled, ashamed. My Sunday picnics with the Gonzales family, my visits to their home—they became exercises in joy and self-loathing. And I was always particularly careful to position myself on the other side of the aisle, two rows behind the Gonzales family, when they attended our Sunday Mass, so as to have an unrestricted view of Rosa. She always wore this lacy mantilla during Mass that sent me into a frenzy, the way it framed her little face.

These were grievous, grievous sins, my looking at her, thinking about her, telling myself countless stories about our escape together from the world of parents, priests, proscriptions. But I never dared bring them up in Confession; in our isolated little community, the Fathers could recognize everyone's voice.

26

There were moments when I identified with Greg King, even though it was a form of vanity to equate the relatively gentle teasing I got with the suffering he endured, and it was obvious from the way he looked all the time that my unhappiness was a cakewalk compared with his ceaseless nightmare.

I guess it was more sympathy than identification—knowing why people went after him all the time, or understanding how I could make just as good a target as he did.

Like the day in English class when we had to make impromptu speeches on a topic assigned to us on the spot by our classmates. Cub and a couple other guys were the ringleaders: they demanded that King be the first speaker, and they assigned him the topic "The women in my life," with various stipulations designed to force him sexward. You could just feel the excitement in the air—it was like bloodlust. King talking about girls! I can still see him walking up to the front of the classroom, his shoulders rigid, his lips writhing in tension—but at the same time not looking up at Father Ochiltree for help, making no move to get the topic changed, not hesitating to take his punishment. The classroom was alternately hooting and silent in anticipation. Incredible palpable tension. Cub shouting out rules like, "It can't be a mother or a sister! It can't be a nun!" Determinedly trying to cut off all of King's escapes.

And then King turned and said, "My topic is 'The

Women in My Life,' and I would like to start with the most important woman of all: The Blessed Virgin Mary."

At which time the whole class started booing and calling out objections.

But here's the weird part: you could hear a hint of respect in the shouting, detect a trace of affection. Outright admiration. And maybe even relief that King had found a way to deliver us all from our cruelty, our sin.

Δ

There was a group of us who took on a "literary" air—an *hauteur* that had us trading paperbacks, carrying them around showily, reading them, talking about them incessantly during the rare rec periods when we weren't listening to Dylan. We were quite precious—a more-serious-than-thou club of four or five juniors and sophomores trading copies of *Animal Farm, 1984, A Tree Grows in Brooklyn, The Catcher in the Rye, The Fountainhead,* and *Atlas Shrugged.* It was a mark of sophistication to have read those six books, to be seen with them. Particularly *Atlas Shrugged,* which ran to some 1300 pages—its bulk a tangible sign of the reader's seriousness.

That's pretty much all that was memorable about Rand's two books: their length and the occasional graphic sex scene. None of us had ever come across such a thing. These scenes were even more shocking, thrilling, than the "terrific fart" Edgar Marsalla laid in chapel in *The Catcher in the Rye.* And they cast serious doubt on what Father Foster had told us in that unforgettable lecture.

Δ

There was a literary touch that year to the badinage as well. My confreres could always get a laugh by suddenly saying, apropos of nothing, some purported author/title combination, setting off a session in which two or three of us would just keep tossing them back and forth:

"*Yalu River*, by I.P. Freely."
"*Under the Bleachers*, by Seymour Butts."
"*Blood in the Saddle*, by the Kotex Kid."

Δ

English II	B
Latin II	B
Geometry	B
History II U.S.	B
Sacred Doctrine II	B
Speech	A
Typing	C

27

Every year, as soon as everyone got back from Christmas break, the seminary put on a big theatrical production. Months went into rehearsal, parents helped with costuming and stage construction, seminarians played all the parts, male and female, and every seminarian, whether in the production or not, got caught up in the excitement. My freshman year I was a humble stagehand, but I got a speaking/singing part this time around: Eulalie MacKechnie Shinn in *The Music Man*.

They announced the roles at lunch one day, and I let out a piercing squeal. I was the most excited soul in the refectory.

Δ

There was no joking around, no teasing, about those of us who were going to be dressing up and performing as women. Even the obvious fact that we could make credible women went unremarked. I kept looking through the cast and seeing how each seminarian had characteristics similar to those of the character he was playing: You could easily picture Mark Reilly as Harold Hill, Terry Muller (the only rookie in the cast) as Marian the Librarian—pretty little Terry was the new favorite "so soft and fine" target of Don Kalvin. It seemed that for every one of us, the character he was picked to play was sort of a caricature of the actor himself. It really was remarkable.

But me as Eulalie MacKechnie Shinn? I didn't get

it, but everybody else sure seemed to. And I was too happy to be in the play to think about it much.

Δ

Alma: Pick a little, talk a little, pick a little, talk a little, cheep cheep cheep, talk a lot, pick a little more

Alma and Ethel: Pick a little, talk a little, pick a little, talk a little, cheep cheep cheep, talk a lot, pick a little more

All the ladies: Pick a little, talk a little, pick a little, talk a little, cheep cheep cheep, talk a lot, pick a little more

Maud: Professor, her kind of woman doesn't belong on any committee.

Of course, I shouldn't tell you this but she advocates dirty books.

Harold: Dirty books?!

Alma: Chaucer

Ethel: Rabelais

Eulalie: Balzac!

Maud: And the worst thing

Of course, I shouldn't tell you this but—

Alma: I'll tell.

Ethel: The man lived on my street, let me tell.

Eulalie: Stop! I'll tell.

She made brazen overtures to a man who never had a friend in this town till she came here.

Alma: Oh, yes
That woman made brazen overtures
With a gilt-edged guarantee
She had a golden glint in her eye
And a silver voice with a counterfeit ring
Just melt her down and you'll reveal
A lump of lead as cold as steel
Here, where a woman's heart should be!

Eulalie, Ethel, Maud, Alma, Mrs Squires:
He left River City the Library building
But he left all the books to her

Alma: Chaucer

Ethel: Rabelais

Eulalie: Bal-zac!

Ladies: Pick a little, talk a little, pick a little, talk a little,
cheep cheep cheep, talk a lot, pick a little more
Pick a little, talk a little, pick a little, talk a little,
cheep cheep cheep, talk a lot, pick a little more
Pick a little, talk a little, pick a little, talk a little,
Cheep cheep cheep cheep cheep cheep cheep cheep
Cheep cheep cheep cheep cheep cheep cheep cheep
Cheep cheep cheep cheep cheep cheep cheep cheep
Pick a little, talk a little, cheep!

Δ

I was resolved to steal the show with my "Ballll ... zac!"

Δ

We practiced every day after class, working on our lines, working our way through the songs, the routines, learning, refining. Aiming toward the first dress rehearsal late in spring.

28

We had just more or less hit our stride with rehearsals when we took a week off for a sojourn at Yosemite National Park. I was completely unprepared for the grandeur we encountered there, its effect on the soul. The Spectacle. A deep silence the likes of which I'd never heard before. It was overwhelming—all you could think about, walking around in that place, hiking, climbing, staring, was God. It was as religious as I'd felt since entering the seminary.

Δ

We stayed in cabins arranged in facing rows with a wide path down the middle. The cabins were on short stilts, with a set of four steps leading up to their front doors. There were four of us in each one. We got all our dishes and bedding from a central storage warehouse and lugged everything back to where we'd be living. Mike Rainier, Greg King, Bob Dolan and I shared our cabin; I felt kind of secretly embarrassed at how excited I was to be setting up house with Bob...one of those "Is this a weird 'particular friendship'?" moments I was having more and more frequently.

Δ

It took a few hours to get everything in place, after which we started banging on each others' doors, gathering a crowd to go exploring. We kept knocking on Jim Winfrey's cabin door—he and Greg McLeod and a couple other guys we wanted to come along with us were setting up in there—but they wouldn't open the door, which they'd locked. We kept banging and banging and yelling at them to come out.

Finally, Bob yelled, "What are you guys doing?"

Winfrey yelled back: "We're taking turns shitting on each other's chests so we can see our assholes move."

Δ

We went back to our cabin to wait. We left the door open; then Rainier for some reason got up and slammed it shut, apparently forgetting that we'd left it open on purpose. It happened that Winfrey was coming up the stairs just then and had grabbed the doorjamb as he came up the last step, so the door slammed on his knuckles.

He kicked the door open and stepped into the room, his face beet-red the way only his could get. He gave Rainier The Stare—the blazing blue eyes in that sea of red that was his Control Your Body face—and said, "God damn your soul to Hell, Rainier. May God damn your soul for eternity to the fires of Hell." In that frightening deep rich robotic voice that was so eerily chilling. "May God damn your soul…." Over and over again. Rainier just stared at him, terrified, waiting for Winfrey to start laughing. But Winfrey just kept staring right back, looking infinitely furious.

He had this way not only of making you uncertain as to whether he was joking, but also of making you feel that he had powers of some kind, that he really could arrange to have your soul damned for eternity to Hell. None of us knew what to do.

We found ourselves feeling really uneasy, a little scared, not knowing where Winfrey was going with all this.

Then he turned around and walked out, with that pigeon-toed gait that only served to add to everyone's unease whenever he came around.

"Goll," Bob said after he was gone, and a shaken Rainier had stepped outside as well. "Jim was really getting into it there." He looked scared—like he'd seen something from the spiritual world that he couldn't handle.

Δ

Apparently we were visiting Yosemite during an offseason. We were the only people there—a marvelous feeling. There was deep snow almost everywhere, the rivers were swollen, rapid, full of newly melted snow, and it was relatively cold. And we had to stay in at night because bears would come sauntering down the path between our cabins after the sun went down, knocking over garbage cans in a businesslike manner. It was pretty much their park once it got dark.

29

I developed this inexplicable suspicion that Winfrey was guiding us spiritually, slowly taking away our faith. Even now, I can't say how he did it, or why I felt that way at the time. But there's no question that he exerted a tremendous power over all of us. And that his anger had something to do with how we all were gradually losing faith not only in our vocations, but in Catholicism, even in God Himself. That the world that had coddled us so thoroughly before we entered the seminary—a world that had an easy answer for everything and left no room for doubt about why we were alive here on earth and where we were headed—began to fall away the day we entered the seminary. I reacted with fear and denial; Winfrey reacted with rage.

Δ

By which I mean, regarding loss of faith: It was more a gradual wearing away, a growing disillusionment. There was no sense of holiness in the seminary, no sense that I was surrounded by saints the way I'd dreamed I would be. It's one thing to notice it in your fellow seminarians, but another to notice it in the Fathers, how they seem so ordinary, so human, with more weaknesses than they should have. And if they don't—that is, if they do have that aura of holiness like Brother Fred did—it just ends up giving you the creeps.

Δ

That's kind of the way it was that whole second year.

We were much more aware of departures among the upperclassmen, and those departures seemed much more numerous. Doubts about our vocations, doubts even that vocations were worthwhile, seemed always on our minds.

Δ

From this temporal distance, it seems obvious that what was going on with us, in our little place, was going on throughout the church. Vatican II ended that year, and with it came the end of the Latin Mass—a relief to us all, something for which American Catholics had been agitating for years. But in retrospect, that seems to have been just another of those little disillusionments. For all of our excitement over changing the ritual of the Mass, introducing folk music, conducting the service in English, surrounding the altar instead of sitting in pews staring at the priest's back—in general making the Mass more intimate and informal, more real—there was also an underlying sense of unease and confusion. If these rituals, this language, meant nothing, what about everything else? There was a feeling among all of us that everything in Church tradition was suddenly open to question. For all of our pretensions to rebellion and commitment to change, it was unnerving.

Δ

This was all wrapped up in big changes on the seminary grounds as well. The new monastery was finished and ready for the Fathers to move in. This meant that the four upper classes would move in to the former Fathers' quarters in the building overlooking the ballfields, right across a little square from the classroom building, and that the dorm, now housing only the rookie and sophomore classes, would no longer have bunk beds. Those in the upper classes would live two to a room.

The new monastery was gorgeous. A spacious sacristy, with a locked vault for the chalices. A splendid main altar under a stylish stained-glass canopy in the middle of a large chapel. The chapel was encircled by an aisle; there were altars in little niches lined along three branches of the aisle, with the fourth opening into the sacristy.

It was very cool, very modern—pebble flooring, stylish abstract/religious designs on the walls and in the stained glass. People came from all over the Bay Area to tour, to pray, to have private masses. The old adobe-walled seminary buildings looked terribly drab by comparison.

30

The ebbing of faith was a matter of little things making big impressions—sometimes subconsciously—each one driving your disillusionment up a notch.

Like one morning, serving Mass for Father Lester on one of the side altars in the new monastery. Each night, the sacristan would lay out vestments for next morning's masses—fourteen sets of vestments for the fourteen altars. Each Father would say his own mass at one of the side altars, with a single seminarian serving as his altar boy. The Fathers would let their designated servers know the night before what time next morning they wanted to say Mass; most of the masses were said at around the same time— 7:00.

Father Lester always wanted to say Mass earlier than any of the others. He had me come down this particular morning at 6:00—we were the only two there. Apparently he always did this—it was just that this was the only time I was the one called to serve him.

He whispered his way with shocking speed through the service, muttering his prayers barely loud enough for me to hear and utter my responses. He didn't even stop to wait for my responses, really, or ever slow down even a little, until we got to Communion.

I brought the cruets up to him, the water and wine, to pour into his chalice. Most priests had you pour in most of the cruet of water, and only a drop of wine. But Father

Lester stopped the water—he put his finger under the lip of the cruet and pushed it gently up—after just a drop had fallen into the chalice. Then when I put the same amount of wine in and made as if to withdraw, he reached out wordlessly with a finger and pressed the mouth of the cruet down until all the wine had been poured out.

After he drank the hurriedly-made-Sacred Blood, the Mass slowed down to a proper pace.

Δ

THE PRIESTHOOD TO ME
By Loel Miller

What does the priesthood mean to me? Why am I spending thirteen years of my life preparing for this vocation? Why am I willing to give up many of the things a normal boy my age wants to have?

To me, the priesthood means offering Christ to His Father in that sublime mystery of the Mass. It means bringing souls close to Christ through Baptism and Confession. It means feeding Christ's flesh to souls in Holy Communion. In other words, being a priest to me means doing Christ's work now, in the Twentieth Century.

Why am I spending thirteen years of my life preparing for my vocation? If this is the greatest of all vocations for a human being, then thirteen years is not enough time to prepare anyone for it. Even if a person should spend the rest of life at it he would not be fully prepared to take up completely the duties of a second Christ.

Why do I want to give up the things a normal boy

my age would have? For all the material good that I seem to be giving up, I am getting back happiness and peace of mind a thousandfold. The joy, the comfort, the security of living close to God makes the sacrifice easy to bear. And for all of the duties that I will have to perform as a priest, I will get a torrent of graces from God in return and great satisfaction in dealing with the people I will serve. To get anything in life, you must give up something in return. The more you are willing to give up, the more you will get in return. What are material rewards that I might have for seventy or eighty years, when God will reward even the smallest sacrifices that I make in His name...forever!

31

The dorm with the upper classes gone and all the upper bunks taken down looked massive and oddly empty. The ceilings seemed cathedral-high, there were weird new echoes, and you could see all the way across the room.

I wonder sometimes if the spaciousness, or maybe just the sudden change, was a factor in Greg King's breakdown. Two or three nights after the move, I was awakened in the middle of the night by screams. I got up and ran over to where a group was gathered in one corner, and when I got over there I saw that King was up on top of the lockers, screaming. He didn't seem aware that any of us were there—I heard Cub say that he thought Greg was sleepwalking. Father Simpson finally came, then some other Fathers came, and Father Simpson ended up climbing up there and wrapping King in a bear hug, basically, until he came out of it.

He wasn't in class the next day, and we found out at dinner that he was gone and not coming back.

Δ

That's the way it was with a lot of the departures. Not that people had these breakdowns all that often, but that they just suddenly would not be there. And you'd find out afterward that they were gone, and you'd never really know whether they decided to leave, had to leave, or what. The Fathers never explained those things to us—ever. And we were eager not to know.

Δ

But then again there would also be a different kind of departure—like Richard—Retard—Hudson's. No less sudden, no less explosive, no less scary.

We had just gotten out of *Music Man* rehearsals and were standing around outside the auditorium when we saw him come walking down the hill really fast. And when he got close enough for us to see his face, we could see that he was furious.

He came right up to us, stopped, and said, "I'm quitting. Leaving the seminary." This came as quite a shock—not because he was one of the more devout seminarians, which he was, but because there wasn't even the remotest chance that he could survive on the outside. I mean, he was damaged—even worse than King, in some ways—and the idea that he had decided on his own to leave just wasn't credible. But then if it wasn't his decision, what could he have done to make the Fathers kick him out? And why did he say "quitting"?

Now he just lost it and started shouting. "There's a lot of hungry women out there, and I'm going to get my share! A lot of hungry women out there! Waiting for me! Hungry women! Hungry women!" He just wouldn't stop with the "hungry women" business.

His eyes were kind of blank—unblinking, blazing, weirdly expressionless. It was scary. "There's a lot of hungry women out there waiting, and I'm going to get my share!"

All you could feel was deep sadness. I mean, he was

one of those people—like me—that you could never imagine with a girl.

We finally just started drifting off, one by one. None of us could think of anything to say.

I don't know when he left, exactly...all I know is that he wasn't there the next morning.

Δ

It was hard not to notice how often I was the butt of a certain kind of joke among my confreres. Always signaling what they thought of me. Like when Don Vogel came up to me, in front of five or six others, and said, "Fred! I had a nightmare last night...I dreamt that I was Jayne Mansfield's new baby—and she decided to bottlefeed me."

Everybody roared...as did I. Then Vogel said, "Do you get it? Do you know why it's funny?" And everybody stood there staring at me accusingly. As if I couldn't possibly have understood the joke.

And to be honest, I wasn't entirely sure I did.

32

The Gonzales family, apparently oblivious to my fixation with Denny's sister, loved having me over to their house. They had Denny bring me home whenever the seminary allowed it. I would sit at their kitchen table and devour everything his mom set anywhere near me. She was thrilled at my gluttony—I think she felt like she was saving the life of a starving orphan. She kept talking about how she needed to put meat on my bones, how skinny I was, and how flattered she was that I adored her cooking.

At some point they ran out of food, or called an end to the meal or something, and Denny and his sister and I went out to the living room to sit down while Denny and I gathered our strength to go outside and run around his neighborhood.

But then Denny's mom called him back into the kitchen, and Rosa and I were suddenly sitting there alone. I couldn't think of a word to say…I just sat there glancing at her, looking away, glancing at her, looking away, terrified, trying to hide my terror, sure that my sin would become so obvious to her that I'd be thrown out of their house forever.

Denny's youngest brother—I think he was about two—came toddling out and climbed up into Rosa's lap, reached out without warning and slapped her hard, right on her breast. Then he turned and did something a two-year-old couldn't possibly know how to do: leered at me.

Poor Rosa was terribly embarrassed. And I was

scared. I sat there trying to figure out where to look, what to do. And wondering how obvious my problem must be if a two-year-old could see it. Or was he some unwitting agent of God, sent to send me a warning?

Δ

My various Rosa fantasies, which assailed me constantly—in class, in the rec room, in chapel, in bed at night—almost always involved flight culminating in my ruin. My reputation, my dreams, my life destroyed by my love for her. It wasn't until years afterward that I noticed the running theme: to truly, fully, love a woman meant destroying your life because of her. Submitting happily to ruination. No sexual fantasy in those days was complete without self-destruction.

I wonder now if it was the Bible speaking to me, through those fantasies…casting me as Adam, Rosa as Eve. The temptress, promising everything, destroying everything, opening the door to unknown pleasures so violent, so compelling, so infinitely satisfying as to be worth the loss of everything that matters, even Paradise.

But leading first of all to shame, to secrecy, to hiding, to isolation. A condition not all that different from life in the seminary, vis-à-vis the outside world.

Δ

One of the privileges of being a sophomore was a weekly outing to a radio station, where four of us went into a sound studio and recited the rosary for a program called "Radio Rosary," which was broadcast live. I was terribly earnest about this program, terrified of slipping up during the group recitation of the Hail Marys and Lord's Prayers, and particularly terrified of my solos.

At the beginning of each decade, the soloist would step out from the kneeling group and recite that decade's "mystery" into the microphone, as in, "The First Sorrowful Mystery: The Agony in the Garden." The idea was that listeners were supposed to meditate on the mystery during the recitation of the ensuing decade—that set of one Lord's Prayer and ten Hail Marys, one of five such sets that make up the Rosary.

How I managed to speak through my heart-pounding terror of stammering or otherwise screwing up, I'll never know. But for all the times I did that program, I never managed to calm down, get over my fear.

Δ

The First Joyful Mystery: The Annunciation.
The Second Joyful Mystery: The Visitation.
The Third Joyful Mystery: The Nativity.
The Fourth Joyful Mystery: The Presentation.
The Fifth Joyful Mystery: The Finding of Jesus in the Temple.

Δ

My Bob Dolan problem was growing uncomfortably obvious to my confreres. Greg McLeod particularly delighted in silent little teasing gestures, like moving from my right side to my left, so as to insinuate himself between Bob and me, on our evening walks up and down the hill, giving me a broad mocking smile as he wedged in between us. And on outings, when Bob and I started walking off together, we'd hear our confreres yelling after us, "Clique! Clique!"— shorthand for "particular friendship!"

Δ

I knew—sensed, at any rate—that something "wrong" lay at the center of this friendship, but I consistently turned away from examining it. Our bond just had too much meaning to me, and "meaning" trumped everything. That was the extent of my examination of conscience on the matter.

33

During my constant listening to his albums, I came to regard Dylan as a modern-day Biblical figure—a prophet, a Gospel writer. His lyrics kept ringing familiarly with sentiments, values, lines that seemed taken directly from the Bible and turned into modern-day religious instruction: "For the loser now / Will be later to win," "The line it is drawn / The curse it is cast / The slow one now / Will later be fast".… And a marvelous tendency to speak in parable—"How many seas must a white dove sail / Before she can sleep in the sand?" This seemed particularly so in "A Hard Rain's A-Gonna Fall," to which we listened almost constantly, committing it to memory—no small feat, given the length of that song. "I saw a highway of diamonds with nobody on it / I saw a black branch with blood that kept drippin'," "I saw a white ladder all covered with water." Powerful religious images, to our minds. Old and New Testamentesque. And through it all the mood and vision of an Apocalypse—it struck a powerful chord with us, the combination of hipness and Catholicism. We never sat around trying to understand anything specific by way of meaning in these lines; all we cared about was their emotional power, the power of the visions they inspired, the mood that came over us when we listened to him singing/declaiming/ preaching.

He made righteousness so cool at a time when we were embarrassed about our own religious feelings, religious beliefs, earnestness. He was the kind of evangelist we all imagined ourselves becoming, in the New Church brought about by our generation—revolutionaries determined to make God and religion relevant to people who were falling away, for good reason, from the traditional church.

Δ

The First Sorrowful Mystery: The Agony in the Garden.
The Second Sorrowful Mystery: The Scourging at the Pillar.
The Third Sorrowful Mystery: The Crowning with Thorns.
The Fourth Sorrowful Mystery: The Carrying of the Cross.
The Fifth Sorrowful Mystery: The Crucifixion.

Δ

We were growing more and more aware of a profound generation gap even within the seminary walls. There were a few juniors who were as devoted to Dylan as were my friends and I, but the upper classes just didn't get him. The only upperclassman I knew who evinced any passion for music of any kind was a very cool guy, a widely respected fourth-year student named Oscar Rodriguez. And he was obsessed with Barbra Streisand.

You'd look in his room and see her albums arrayed upright, facing into the room, along his windowsill, on his desk against the wall: *The Barbra Streisand Album; The Second Barbra Streisand Album; The Third Album; Funny Girl; People; My Name is Barbra; My Name is Barbra, Two.* You wanted to mock him, but Rodriguez was a really cool guy, so you couldn't. All you could do was wonder what the deal was. It was legitimately baffling—Dylan's power seemed so obvious to us that we couldn't understand why he wasn't the only singer everybody listened to. And Streisand? You couldn't be any more square than she was.

34

The seminary sat in a rough part of Oakland—particularly down at the far end, where a locked cyclone gate separated the seminary grounds from a short road leading to an Oakland neighborhood where there was always something noteworthy going on. I used to sneak down there, climb the gate, and walk out to where I could see the action. Most nights I would just look for a minute or two, then flee back to the safety of the seminary grounds.

One night a pack of Hells Angels came roaring down the street, taking up the whole road—including the lanes for opposing traffic. The roar was prodigious, the bikers huge, hairy, filthy, frightening.

They were headed for a house directly across the street from where I was standing. They milled around there, drinking beer from cans, many of them still straddling the bikes they'd ridden up onto the dirt yard, occasionally revving their engines.

I was riveted by the women who'd ridden in with them: grimy, with long, dirty hair, wearing little clothing, they pranced and preened through the chaos, looking simultaneously exciting, sinful, thoroughly degraded, and delighted with themselves.

Δ

I would scour San Francisco and Oakland newspapers in search of Hells Angels stories, of which there were a good number. Their leader, Sonny Barger, was particularly quotable. "I don't understand why they keep making up stories about us," he said in one, complaining about news coverage. "Isn't the truth bad enough?" I couldn't stop thinking about that quote—it seemed to me that there was something deliberately mocking, mischievously indecipherable about it.

Δ

For weeks, I went back down there almost nightly, after lights out. I'd sneak out of the dorm, down the hill, over the gate, hoping to get another glimpse of the gang and those women. But the only thing anywhere near that exciting happened one night when a little group of prostitutes standing on the corner where I emerged started yelling at me: "Hey! Short-pants!" "Hey! Where you goin', short-pants!" Vying with one another to deliver the best line: "How about a case of the jitters!" "Got a sweet trap here for that one-eyed trouser mouse of yours!" "How about a big ol' taste of my sugar britches here?" Hooting at my humiliation when I fled.

35

We were getting to the point in our *Music Man* rehearsals now where we were working on costumes and makeup, doing quasi-dress rehearsals. It was incredibly exciting the way the show was coming together. I don't think any of us performing had expected it to be as credible as it was shaping up to be. I know I never expected to be as credible a mayor's wife as I was turning out to be.

Various moms were the volunteer wardrobe and makeup experts, and they seemed to take these jobs as seriously as if they were working on a real Broadway production. They did all kinds of work on our dresses and wigs at home, and they'd bring this stuff in and sit with us for hours, putting on our makeup, adjusting our costumes, fooling around with our wigs.

I had the misfortune of having a mom assigned to me who was gorgeous. She'd be running her hands over my gowns, putting on my makeup or working on my wig, her face right up against mine, her hands conferring the softest touch imaginable. I'd close my eyes when she was working me over, partly to keep from staring at her and partly so I could concentrate on the sweet soft sound of her breathing.

She was completely absorbed in her task—me. I was alternately thrilled, ashamed, thrilled, ashamed.... On the days I knew we were having dress rehearsals, I'd be looking forward to her arrival for hours. And afterwards, thinking how for her it was probably like playing with dolls, I'd feel like a fool.

I'd picture her wide dark eyes only inches away from mine, and think how fortunate it was that I was wearing a voluminous gown. And wonder if I was the worst sinner in the history of sin.

Δ

Only two days after my latest close encounter with my makeup mom, I was standing with Bob and Greg out on the turnaround that looks down on the ballfields when Father Simpson came out to chat with us for a while. Somehow we ended up talking about the vow of celibacy, and the conduct of priests around women. "It's just fortunate that we wear cassocks," he said. "We walk around with hard-ons all the time...I'd rather they not be noticeable."

Δ

The First Glorious Mystery: The Resurrection.
The Second Glorious Mystery: The Ascension.
The Third Glorious Mystery: The Descent of the Holy Spirit.
The Fourth Glorious Mystery: The Assumption.
The Fifth Glorious Mystery: The Coronation.

Δ

Jesus does not permit the sinless body of His Mother to decay in the grave.

Δ

With our second year nearly over, it finally came time for the gala performance of *The Music Man*. The auditorium was packed with families, seminarians, Fathers.

Backstage was a madhouse, with the mothers fussing over our hair and makeup, people running every which way. Incredible excitement, tension.

I was nervous enough about my performance not to be distracted by the mom's allure. All I cared about—aside from watching to see how Mark Reilly would get through singing love songs to Terry Muller in front of a full auditorium—was getting through "Pick a Little, Talk a Little" and getting a laugh with my most important line: "Ballll...zac!"

I kept pacing around backstage, saying it over and over to myself. Varying the intonation, deepening the voice, playing out that first syllable at various lengths, looking for the perfect comic touch.

And when my time came, I brought down the house. I was pretty sure I was the audience favorite—that, at any rate, was how I chose to interpret the outsized laughter that erupted whenever I delivered my lines.

36

For the last two weeks or so of the seminary year, you start dreading having to go home. This time, the second time around, was much worse—it seemed like there was more to hide, and more to miss. You'd think that going back out into the world would be an escape to a freer place, but it turned out to be the opposite: the place where we felt freest now was in here.

This year, there was something else lurking in the depths—this sense that our little insulated world wasn't sustainable for much longer. All those Dylan lyrics about the old order rapidly fading and the hard rain that was coming and how staying where we were just wasn't an option— "You better start swimmin' or you'll sink like a stone"—had us figuratively looking over our shoulders all the time. And realizing what a safe place—what a retreat—we'd found here.

And we were starting to say out loud things that had secretly been on my mind—on our minds—for months. Doubts about the worth of a vocation; doubts about Church leaders; doubts about the legitimacy of the institutional Church. It was one thing to carry these things around in your head, but a considerably more frightening thing to be talking out loud about them and to discover that they weren't on your mind alone.

I didn't want to have to give up the life—the freedom from family strictures, the freedom from girls—that this haven gave me. But I kept having to admit to myself that I was living an ever-greater lie. And one day when Mark Reilly and I were having a serious conversation about all this, he—with great hesitation, almost terror—said, "I don't know if I even believe in God anymore."

Δ

The day before we scattered for our homes, I was sitting in the empty refectory with Bob Dolan, who was really glum. "Do you know what people call us?" he asked.

"No." It was true—I had no idea that we'd been nicknamed.

"Freddio and Robbiette."

Δ

So great is His anguish that His sweat becomes as drops of blood falling to the ground.

Δ

English II	A
Latin II	C
Geometry	B
History II U.S.	A
Sacred Doctrine II	B
Speech	A
Hist. Am. Instr.	A

37

Through a friend of his, my Dad had lined up a summer job for me with the Bellingham Park Department. I spent eight hours a day with a set of clippers in my hand, trimming the grass around the tombstones in Bayview Cemetery. A good summer of reading—my favorite tombstone was for someone named Henry Stiff.

My coworkers were fulltime park department employees. Hardscrabble guys. We would sit in the cemetery's equipment shed at lunchtime and listen to Paul Harvey on the radio while we "strapped on the feedbag." I may have gone through the whole summer without saying a word to anyone there. These guys swore, told dirty jokes, used racial slurs…I was terrified of them finding out I was a seminarian.

Δ

I stayed away from old schoolmates, playmates, neighbors. I went to Church on Sunday; worked during the week; and drove my father to the brink of madness by playing Dylan on the living-room stereo all summer long. He was a big fan of Peter, Paul and Mary, and loved their versions of Dylan's songs, but he found the sound of Dylan's voice—which he'd never heard before—unbearable. I showed him—just because I knew it would set him off— the liner notes where Dylan wrote that his songs weren't so much songs as "exercises in tonal breath control."

Dad didn't think the subject was all that funny. He'd

come back from an outing on any given Sunday afternoon and find me sitting on the living room couch, looking out the picture window, with my three Dylan albums arrayed on the windowsill. Listening, listening, listening to that horrible rasping angry voice.

Δ

I remember pretty much nothing else from that summer other than hearing from my mom that Myra Kepler—the third-most beautiful girl in my class at Assumption—had dropped out of high school and gone to beauty school, thereby establishing herself as the most scandalous figure in the Assumption Church community.

I saw her at Mass once that summer, going up the side aisle to receive Communion. She had a massive bouffant hairdo—it was purple—and she looked worldly beyond our years.

38

Moving out of the common dorm and into the Fathers' old quarters was a very big deal, it turned out. We suddenly felt like college students instead of high-school kids. Two to a room—Denny Gonzales and I were room-mates—in a two-story wing with capacious bathrooms and showers, two big new recreation rooms—one with a television, the other, up in a tower, with a big stereo—carpeted halls, a balcony, and a view from our room directly over a forested canyon.

The whole setup made us feel elite. And entitled to think for ourselves, question everything we'd been taught. The Fathers more or less abetted us in this, probably because they were doing a lot of questioning, rethinking, of their own. The whole Church institution—the authoritarian part of it, at any rate—seemed to have lost its hold over everyone. We—Fathers and seminarians alike—started to feel that we could set our own rules, make up our own Church, redefine our creed. Tear everything down and start over, building a new and newly relevant modern Church.

Δ

I took up with a new social circle, being careful to stay as far away as possible from Bob Dolan. We didn't exchange so much as a word for the rest of our time in the seminary.

Δ

We were surrounded—and enchanted—by New Thinking: Joan Baez had a peace institute in nearby Monterey; Esalen, also nearby, was promoting Peace and Love; City Lights Books was across the bay in San Francisco; the Free Speech Movement had taken over in Berkeley; Greg Vernon, a senior and my new guru, had a subscription to *Ramparts* Magazine, which we read religiously. And we were all resolutely opposed to the Vietnam War.

Δ

We got into the writings of the French theologian Pierre Teilhard de Chardin, especially his *The Phenomenon of Man*—another of those books we would brandish to show off our seriousness. We felt that he'd found a way forward for Catholics in the way he melded his faith with Darwinism, and especially in his argument that evolution was steadily progressive and that therefore we were evolving toward an "Omega point"—a state of higher consciousness toward which human consciousness was evolving just as physical life was evolving into a better set of creatures. Eventually, humans would be something like angels, as we understood it.

There was no question but that we were to be the new wave of Catholicism and that the old Vatican-directed church was dying out. The fact that the Vatican's Sacred Congregation of the Holy Office had issued a reprimand—called a "monitum"—entitled *Warning Considering the Writings of Father Teilhard de Chardin* struck us as pretty hilarious. It gave him all the more cachet, as far as we were concerned. To all of us—even the Fathers—the Vatican had become a joke.

Δ

Denny kept a portrait of his family on his desk.

Δ

My contribution to the room décor was a shrine to Joan Baez. We had made what amounted to a religious pilgrimage to a concert of hers at the Cow Palace—an amazing event. A full house, everyone in thrall to a lone woman with an acoustic guitar. Other than a stool for her, a little table with a drinking glass, and her microphone, the stage was bare.

The song that brought the house down most— among a slew of crowd-pleasers—was Dylan's "With God on Our Side," a song we'd listen to daily, both her rendition and Dylan's. Those lines, "Though they murdered six million / in the ovens they fried / The Germans now too / have God on their side," had us shaking our heads in weary wisdom, looking meaningfully at one another, every single time we heard it.

Δ

When the concert ended, Vernon and McLeod and I just sat there, stunned, in awe. No one among the thousands there was getting up to leave.

It was a good long time before people started filing out. I looked around for signs of security guards or ushers, saw no one, ran up to the stage, grabbed Baez's drinking glass, and fled.

Safely back home, I found an old bookcase with a

glass-fronted top shelf down in our building's cellar. The glass door was hinged at the top. I took it up to our room and made my little shrine in that top compartment: the water glass, the concert program, and the album cover for *Joan Baez in Concert, Part 2*. A few weeks later I was able to add a letter I'd gotten from her, in reply to one I'd sent after seeing her in concert. "One of the reasons I wrote back to you," it said, "was that you didn't ask for anything—not even a reply." I'd carefully planned that, on the theory that it was the only chance I had of getting an answer.

Δ

Admonition

Several works of Fr. Pierre Teilhard de Chardin, some of which were posthumously published, are being edited and are gaining a good deal of success.

Prescinding from a judgement about those points that concern the positive sciences, it is sufficiently clear that the above-mentioned works abound in such ambiguities and indeed even serious errors, as to offend Catholic doctrine.

For this reason, the most eminent and most revered Fathers of the Holy Office exhort all Ordinaries as well as the superiors of Religious institutes, rectors of seminaries and presidents of universities, effectively to protect the minds, particularly of the youth, against the dangers presented by the works of Fr. Teilhard de Chardin and of his followers.

Given at Rome, from the palace of the Holy Office,

on the thirtieth day of June, 1962.

Sebastianus Masala, Notarius

Δ

That year was to feature a series of lectures by visiting Redemptorist Fathers who had been off in the foreign missions or studying in Rome. Generally, the presentations belittled Church tradition, calling into question the worth or meaning of everything from Papal Infallibility to the sacraments.

We laughed with the Father who told us that "hearing nuns' confessions is like being bombarded with popcorn." To my mind, nothing more highlighted the point that Confession was an empty ritual.

Which in my case was a convenient stance, since I'd stopped going to Confession almost a year earlier. I kept telling myself it was irrelevant and pointless, although the real reason I'd stopped going was the lack of any Fathers available to hear Confession who wouldn't recognize my voice; I just couldn't take the embarrassment of being recognized in the confessional anymore.

Δ

We leapt to our feet one day and gave the visiting lecturer a standing ovation when he concluded his rousing argument that the Transubstantiation was metaphorical rather than actual with, "I am an Existentialist, gentlemen! This is bread! This is wine!"

39

I was now part of a "serious" crowd, mostly of seminarians a year ahead of me, who were reading Sartre and Camus, calling ourselves Existentialists, and going out to Berkeley every weekend. We would walk up and down Telegraph Avenue masquerading as UC students, listening (pretty much in vain) for conversations about philosophy, saying "Cool it!" a lot, taking old textbooks to Cody's Books to sell, and coming back with newly purchased used copies of Camus, Sartre, Ferlinghetti, Ginsberg.

Granted, I didn't have even a glimmer of understanding of Ginsberg's poetry. But he hung out with Dylan, so I knew he had to be brilliant, prescient, cool.

Δ

Vernon and I spent countless hours in our new rec room, the top floor in the tower overlooking the little square between our rooms and the classroom building. We arrayed our Dylan albums around the room and listened to them constantly—particularly *Bringing It All Back Home* and *Highway 61 Revisited*. Dylan's move to electric guitar, to rock, was exhilarating and daring—something akin, in our view, to our own break from Rome.

Δ

Oh God said to Abraham, "Kill me a son"
Abe says, "God, you must be puttin' me on"
God say "No." Abe say "What?"
God say, "You can do anything you want Abe, but
The next time you see me comin' you better run"
Well Abe says, "Where you want this killin' done?"
God says, "Out on Highway 61"

40

The seminary population was way down from previous years, with fewer new entrants and with upperclassmen dropping out at pretty furious pace. Vernon's class only had twelve in it—the smallest fourth-year class in the history of the seminary—and our class was down to twenty, also the smallest third-year class in school history.

It gave you this feeling that our way of life was beginning to die out. And it didn't help that the fifth- and sixth-year classes had transferred to St. Mary's College, a few miles away, as part of the Redemptorists' modernization of the seminary.

The idea that post-high-school age students would do better in college than in what Vernon called "six years of high school" seemed enlightened on the surface. But there were girls at St. Mary's. I didn't see how you could lead a truly religious life in a setting like that.

And in general you couldn't help but feel this underlying unease about the change, this conviction that it was only the beginning of something drastic and dangerous, the outright destruction of our little hiding place.

Δ

Vernon and some of his classmates started a new student newspaper, a counterpoint to *The Coastline*, called *the bananafish*—an allusion to our newest hero, J.D. Salinger. I signed on as the typist at first, working my way up to "associate editor."

bananafish was inspired by the underground papers we saw in Berkeley—we saw ourselves as similarly
revolutionary, our mission to shatter the complacency and
intellectual laziness we saw everywhere among our confreres. We signaled our revolutionary aspirations primarily
through refusal to use any upper-case letters.

Δ

the bananafish is a student journal of student opinion; however the opinions expressed therein don't necessarily reflect the views of the editors. the editors welcome your
criticism of either the content or the format of the journal.

Δ

There came over us all this general sense that we
couldn't make things last. You couldn't see the drop-off in
numbers without being forced to think about your own
reasons for being here. And it didn't help that after our
four years here and our ensuing four years at St. Mary's, we
would have to transfer to Wisconsin—as far from California, culturally, as you could imagine.

I finally began acknowledging to myself that I wanted my life to stay the way it was now—living in California,
lightly supervised, protected from my parents, from the
world, pretty much never thinking about anything beyond
the current year. I never pictured myself as a priest anymore.
I never pictured much of anything for myself beyond being
in this place, at this age, assuming that it was leading me
to the life I was intended to live without ever making me
think about exactly what that was, or what I wanted it to be.

Δ

My interest in religious matters was limited to working as many Dylan songs as possible into the daily folk masses that we started holding after we got rid of the Latin Mass.

Δ

The fashion that year was to showily search for Meaning in our lives. With the loss of our faith, however unacknowledged, came a weirdly dreadful void. The general consensus now was that our lives had become purposeless, useless, and that we suffered terribly over our superfluity. At the time, while we were exhilarated by the Vatican II-mandated dropping of the Latin Mass, we also felt a profound (if unacknowledged) loss—of pageantry, of that exotic, God-connected language, of the highly ritualistic and magic nature of the Latin Mass.

The dropping of the ceremonial centerpiece of our faith had me wondering why anything else we'd believed should be any more sacred. Why not drop celibacy? Why prohibit birth control? Why make confession and attendance at Mass mandatory? Why have any rules at all?

Δ

A SEMINARIAN'S FIND
By Rich DeJana

I am finding out what a true Catholic really is. It is surprising to find out how much more your religion means to you, thanks to the new liturgy.

Let's begin at the start of the Mass. The priest enters and second year chanters start the hymn. By the time the hymn is finished the priest begins the Introit (in English) and we all join in. All my life I've read it in my missal, but it always seemed to be something away from the Mass because the celebrant read it in Latin.

The priest returns to the book and reads the Collect in Latin; it still means more than before because the commentator—a man from the fourth year—sums it all up.

Thus continues the Mass until the Offertory, when two of my fellow pupils bring the sacrifices up to the altar. For the first time the people are actually having representatives bring the offerings to the priest.

The next part of the Mass that astounds me is when we say the "Lamb of God" with the priest. This makes me realize the power of the sacrifice.

The last thing that really impresses me, but not the least, is when the priest presents me with Christ and says, "Body of Christ." The joy of eating Christ's Body has always filled me, but I am floored when I see the Host of Christ's Body and then hear the sacred words in my native tongue.

Yes, like many Catholics, I'm beginning to see what a joy and honor being a Catholic is, thanks to the new liturgy.

Δ

Lamb of God, you who take away the sins of the world, have mercy upon us.

Lamb of God, you who take away the sins of the
world, have mercy upon us.
Lamb of God, you who take away the sins of the
world, grant us peace.

Δ

The whole campus seemed caught up in the question of why the seminary—or, for that matter, the institutional Church—existed at all. And if you could question
that, how could you not regard your own presence in the
seminary as anything other than a lie?

Δ

There were times when that seemed to be all we
talked or thought about. In the rookie class that year was
a beautiful, angelic little fair-skinned blond named Bob
Brodie, who was constantly sought after by upperclassmen.
You'd see him every night, walking up and down the road
with two or three older students—one of them almost always Mark Reilly, with whom Brodie often walked alone as
well—all of them unburdening their souls to him, sharing
memories of better days here, going on and on about their
confusion, their unhappiness.

There were nights when I was one of those upperclassmen, overcome with this sensation that Brodie understood better than anyone on earth what I was telling him,
what I was feeling.

Δ

You saw little by way of evidence that the Fathers
noticed any of this, or seemed concerned about our collec-

tive identity crisis. Although Father Simpson did decide to start holding "Encounter Groups" of five or six seminarians each. He held these sessions nightly, pretty much, with each group meeting once a week. We would take turns "sharing," and the others in the group would comment, offer advice or sympathy. The idea was that we were to be completely open in these groups, unafraid. No filtering. And you felt compelled to conjure up distress even if you felt more or less fine. We were all supposed to be deeply unhappy, desperate for understanding. For Meaning.

Father Simpson always prefaced his analysis of your latest unburdening with, "I get the feeling that...." We all picked up that habit, each of us beginning the same way when reacting with sympathy to the one in the center of the Encounter circle: "I get the feeling that...." It was all part of the general ethos that year: that feelings meant everything, that thought was inferior.

41

Early that year, I was appointed sacristan for the Fathers. This was traditionally a high honor, but in my case I was sure the appointment was an attempt at rehabilitation. I interpreted it as a signal that the Fathers were worried about the turn my life had taken—I was skipping classes, sleeping through those I didn't skip, and generally letting it be known through my behavior that I was disaffected, troubled, possibly rebellious.

Δ

It was a big responsibility, being sacristan. I had a key to the safe in which the Fathers kept all the chalices—a tremendous amount of gold of great material value and incalculable spiritual value. I also had a key to the cabinets of sacramental wine—a huge temptation that I resisted, largely out of fear of God-delivered lightning. Every evening after supper, Tim—the other sacristan—and I would go down to lay out the chalices and vestments for the next morning's masses. It was a good two hours' work, much of it painstaking—particularly when you had to carry those chalices around. You had to be very careful not to touch the inside of the cup—the consecrated gold surface that came in contact with the Sacred Blood. Nor could you let your fingers defile the surface on the paten that held the Sacred Body.

Δ

For all of my avowed cynicism, I was terrified of defiling those vessels. I could never tell whether I loved or

Fred Moody

hated that side of myself—that Inner Catholic that couldn't let go of believing.

Δ

Fourteen sets of vestments, laid out according to carefully prescribed ritual, and fourteen six-piece altar vessel sets. For Mass, each Father would don the amice, alb, stole, maniple, cincture, and chasuble—each with its own little prayer. And assembled with the vestments would be the vessels he carried out to the altar for Mass: the chalice, paten, purificator, chalice veil, and the burse with its corporal carefully folded and stored inside it.

Δ

It was disorienting, being the sacristan, feeling both honored and silly every evening.

Δ

Mark and I were down in the sacristy setting up for next morning's masses when we discovered that the purificators made phenomenal Frisbees. I was the first to take one and chuck it at him. Then the war was on. We both armed ourselves with as many as we could carry and chased each other in and out of altar niches, the sacristy, the closet and safe...a real donnybrook. Purificators were flying every which way, and all you could hear was our footsteps and ever-heavier breathing, since even in the heat of battle we were observing Silence, as per our job requirements.

I was about to let fly with another missile when Father Rector suddenly walked into the sacristy. One of Mark's launches flew right by his head, and Father Rector impassively watched it hit the wall behind me. I just stood there with an armful of purificators, terrified, ashamed. There was no misunderstanding what we'd been doing.

Father Rector didn't say a word. He just walked through the sacristy and on into the monastery proper, expressionless. As if Mark and I weren't even there.

We cleaned up hurriedly, finished setting up for Masses, and fled.

We waited for days for the consequence. I expected to be kicked out—what we'd done was that bad.

But nothing was ever said to either of us. Which I finally took as proof positive that the Fathers were fully aware of my various problems and were intent on rehabilitating me.

42

I was never punished for anything, now that I think about it. Never called in to discuss my nonattendance at classes, which was frequent, or my inattention when I was there. We would sit around in our dorm at night, playing music, visiting one another's rooms, and wonder at the ever-loosening discipline. No one seemed to expect much of us other than to show up on time for morning meditation and Mass. The Fathers seemed not only to be indulging our lapses, but actually to be encouraging them.

Δ

Father Simpson was particularly indulgent of everyone, and most particularly indulgent of me. I was spending more and more time with him, joking around, trading books to read, having long and serious conversations about my various problems, preoccupations, pretensions. There didn't seem any longer to be any division between him and me—that is, he didn't seem like an authority figure anymore. He was more like a confidant, a comrade. Someone—like Bob Dolan had been—that I longed to be hanging around with all the time.

Δ

Our Algebra teacher that year was a newly ordained Father whose nickname was Lurch. It was rumored that that had been his nickname in the seminary, and one look at his face told you it had to be true.

He was a good-natured Father, soft-spoken, with a long-suffering air. His eyebrows ran more along the outside of his eyes than above them, giving his face a constantly sad-sack look.

I just could not get into Algebra…it was the only class I hated as much as Latin. It didn't help that the class was the last one of the day, during the heat of the afternoon. I fell into the habit of sitting in the back corner of the classroom, leaning back against the wall, falling into a deep sleep.

Lurch never said a word to me—never tried to wake me, never asked about my nonattendance. It occurred to me that maybe he somehow didn't notice.

But then one afternoon I woke up in an empty classroom, Algebra long over. Lurch had quietly told everyone to sneak out of the room without waking me.

Δ

the halls of hrc
bob Richardson

the halls of h.r.c. echo from the joys of satisfied liberals—over what? the great blessings of more freedoms and—don't forget—more opportunities to develop ourselves, or being able to get out of here once in awhile from it all, including the jerks that are with you three meals a day? isn't it just wonderful? the blessings of liberty of personal responsibility and of course of freedom!

let's argue the matter. pros first.

to begin with, our "new system" is a boon to the priesthood, and to the poor, miserable cloistered seminarian. we are out of the "stone age" into the "modern era." who's whipping themselves over religion anymore? self-sacrifice, a real pain. prayer, just enough to pass with—would christ again have to be crucified today just to get his point across? ah, i almost forgot. we are no longer isolated from the rest of the world. now we too can know the latest hits, fads, and other useful items. our community will be one—who said it wasn't before! and we too develop strongly within. why, we are constantly overflowing with the goodly theme. deep in our hearts, we do believe. we have overcome this day.

now for the cons.

we are losing our sense of values, referring to naturally our main goal—the priesthood. before it was something revered, something holy—worth all the self-sacrifice and sweat we could pour into it. now we won't even endure fifteen minutes of meditation or one decade of a rosary. where is our great drive? we are gradually becoming more self-centered as we reap our harvest of freedoms, privileges, and laxity in christ. religion is under-rated and secondary (at least i hope) to materialism. with it goes our community (or family) spirit—the "kiss my ass" attitude toward all or some.

in conclusion, i firmly advocate a digression to a less emphatic "stone age." i firmly advocate restrictions in areas of weakness and punishments in the form of absence of privileges. you can apply psychology all day long, but the hard hand of authority always gets the point across— straighten up and fly right!

Δ

English III	A
Latin III	C
Algebra 2	C
Civics	B
Biology	C
Sacred Doctrine III	A
Speech II	A

Δ

December 20, 1965

Merry Christmas!

The holiday-vacation fever has hit us hard, and most of the guys are marking off the minutes. They're beginning the Christmas clean-up this evening. There are street-sweepers and window-washers and floor-polishers just about everyplace you look.

Tonight after supper for awhile we're thinking of going caroling around the neighborhood. So far only the choir has been doing much singing of Christmas songs. It's been to three hospitals, an old folks home, and—what proved to be the most enjoyable—a Christmas sing-along with a group of kids from broken homes at the county or-phanage. Tonight the rest of the school will join us as we go around the neighborhood.

There is one morning of classes left which will probably be about as useless endeavor as ever tried. Then tomorrow at noon they'll begin to put the finishing touches on the cleanup, do their packing, and get ready for the

Christmas dinner party. This is to be a chicken dinner affair with half the people in the Bay Area tossing in decorations and extras—thanks to the ingenuity of the junior class who gives the party each year—and to the patience of Mr. Gonzales whose been driving them around to pick up things—and to the Sisters because naturally they got stuck with the cooking —and on and on.

Then early Wednesday morning—some very early—they'll be boarding buses and planes for that long-awaited vacation with you. Here's hoping that you all have a happy Christmas together. God bless you.

Father Simpson

43

GOOD-BYE AND HELLO!
By Tim Lee

Following our return from the Christmas vacation, we were met with the surprising news that our Director, Fr. Foster, was to be transferred to the Alaskan Missions. All of the students here at H.R.C. will feel the College's loss. He had been a man that has made each of the eight-five students feel as if the College was his second home and he their second father. Whether it be on the baseball or football field, in study hall or refectory, he always had time to whip up a hearty joke or two to brighten one's day. If Father wasn't up in his room helping a student with a problem, chances were you would find him down in the garages. There he would be tinkering with one of a number of cars or busses that were continually being reincarnated by his hands. When it seemed as if the studies were just about to bury you under six feet of hard earth, Father would pick you up with an announcement that tomorrow we would be going to a soccer game or on a day's outing. Truly we will miss this man of love in a way that words cannot express.

Moving up the ladder to fill in the vacant spot of Director is Father Simpson. Father is a man who knows all the ropes. Arriving at H.R.C. two years ago, he came as a newly ordained priest to make his year of Tirocinium. Since that time Father has been our Assistant Director, a Latin professor to three different classes, a French instructor, and Director of the choir. He has taken an active part in all of H.R.C.'s recent revivals—from the building of the new monastery to the College Division attending classes at St. Mary's College. As a Director the students can look forward to more stress upon individual responsibilities and more student voice in the government of the College.

Δ

I spent a great many Algebra class periods down at the far end of the seminary grounds, in a field of grasses and daisies overlooking the little creek that ran through the property. I would lie there luxuriating in my lugubriousness, occasionally reading J.D. Salinger short stories or Ferling-hetti or Ginsberg. Mostly I would meditate on my nobility, the profound nature of my suffering, the degree to which I was so much more sensitive and burdened than pretty much anyone else on earth.

Someone like me—tormented, in such agony, so attuned to human suffering—really couldn't be expected to endure classes designed for ordinary students. Anyone could see that it was a waste of my poetic potential—hence the Fathers' reluctance to call me on my behavior.

Δ

in a tiny nitch of night

leon duych

san leandro, California

in a tiny nitch of night,

where all darkness lie there brooding

(breathing comforts rich and warm

petal soft and soothing)

quiet and pure as a peaceful pool,

when perfume bough bend o'er her blooming,

within my soul lie looming.

---

mr. duych is a former member of holy redeemer high school.

Δ

Every other Sunday after Mass, Denny Gonzales and I would walk a mile or so through the neighborhood from the seminary to a Catholic parish church and school, where we would teach Catholic doctrine to Sunday-school kids. On alternate Sundays, Father Simpson would drive us to the Alameda Naval Base, where we would teach kids of Catholic servicemen. Father Simpson was always trusting us with tasks like this, and coming by our room just to talk—about how we were doing, how we thought classmates of ours were doing, what we were reading, what was on our minds.

Δ

I liked the teaching; but if I thought about myself in connection with the priesthood at all now, it was only as a social activist—fighting for civil rights in the South, or against the Vietnam War, or on behalf of California farmworkers. Often Rosa would be working alongside me, the two of us taking on the world, taking on evil together.

44

The first thing we always did when we went on one of our long recreational outings was take off and go hitch-hiking. Davis or Vernon or McLeod and I. We never had a destination in mind—it was mostly about masquerading as people from the real world, seeing if we could get a ride and where it might take us.

Vernon and I were hitchhiking in Monterey one weekend when a souped-up GTO pulled over to pick us up. It was a gleaming, throbbing machine…a common site on California roads in those days, and always exciting. It symbolized freedom and excess, rampant male energy, unlimited expectation.

When we opened the door to get in, the driver looked tough, cool: ducktail haircut, cigarette, tight-fitting T-shirt. As muscled as his car—GTO-worthy, in other words. Nineteen or twenty years old, I guessed. And in the passenger seat was this little babydoll—his girlfriend or wife or whatever, with these big dark eyes, little tiny tight angora sweater, bangs down to her eyes, huge eyelashes. She was like this little confection.

This guy was livin' the dream…I couldn't understand why he stopped to pick us up.

He told us to pile into the back seat and make room for ourselves. It was difficult: the seat was packed with gigantic stuffed animals, all of them pastel-colored. All these gigantic plush cats and bears, bigger than the driver and his girl.

Δ

Mark Reilly and I were alone in my room one night, talking. We were sitting on the floor across from one another. I can't remember what we were talking about—just that it was something relatively serious.

Then all of a sudden we started wrestling. Laughing. And after only a few seconds, maybe as much as a minute, the play turned into something deeply pleasurable, exciting. Nothing like anything I'd ever felt before—deep physical thrilling pleasure.

We stopped, breathless, and resumed our seated positions across from one another. "I'm really embarrassed," Mark said.

"Why?" I asked.

Secretly, though, I knew. I just didn't know how to articulate exactly what it was I knew, what it was that was wrong. I just knew.

45

Dylan came into the Bay Area like a conquering hero that spring. It was like the whole city stopped to deal with his arrival. The press was fascinated—he was on all the TV stations, in all the papers. Story after story about this huge press conference he gave, his answers hilarious, absurd, apparently full of hidden meaning. He played the older reporters for fools, which of course we loved because it felt like he was talking over their heads directly to us. We got it—the reporters were helplessly confused, involuntary straight men.

In all seriousness, he told them that he wasn't a poet—he was a "song-and-dance man"—that he wrote and sang because "I have nothing else to do," and that his favorite current rock group was the Sir Douglas Quintet. Every serious question they asked him was similarly parried. His favorite poets? "W.C. Fields, the family in the circus, Ginsberg, Charlie Rich."

And of course he was asked if he felt like a sell-out for turning from folk to rock. "If I were to sell out," he said this time around, "it would be ladies' garments."

The only time he seemed flummoxed was when Ginsberg suddenly interrupted with a question: "Do you think you'll ever be hung as a thief?"

"You weren't supposed to say that," Dylan answered.

Δ

There were ten or so of us who went to his concert at the Berkeley Community Theater. We had been counting the days to this event for months—Vernon and I were beside ourselves—and before it even started it already had lived up to our expectations. The atmosphere, the crowd…it felt like History.

There we were, the only people our age, surrounded by hipsters and staring down at a front row filled with Hells Angels—our neighbors!—sitting with Allen Ginsberg. Recognizing Ginsberg made us feel very cool and connected, and recognizing the Hells Angels made us feel like outlaws.

Dylan did a two-part concert, the first part his old acoustic songs, the second part his rock act with his new touring band. We felt like we were part of a massive cultural moment, an irreversible shift away from the past, particularly when he played "Ballad of a Thin Man" and "Like a Rolling Stone." And when he threw in some songs we'd not yet heard, we were transported.

It's the way it always was with Dylan: Everything he did felt groundbreaking, profound. You'd constantly be listening and scrutinizing his work for hidden meaning, glimpses of where he was headed next. The whole effect was enhanced for us because of all the religious imagery and intonation in these songs.

And no one was as maddeningly and excitingly elusive as he was. Even his refusal to speak to his audiences during concerts seemed "meaningful."

The only experience I'd ever had that came close to the experience of Dylan was reading the Bible, constantly searching, interpreting, guessing at the inscrutable, the alluring, the fascinating mystery of those texts that filled you with emotions you could never quite find the words to describe, to interpret. He was, for us, similarly oracular, hinting constantly at the Truth.

Δ

I had something of a crisis of conscience after that concert. Realizing how completely different I was now from the child my parents had sent off to the seminary, how much a lie to my family I was living, I wanted to open up to them, tell them who I really was, what was really on my mind. It was very California. I was tired of sending these vapid, deceitful, empty letters home all the time.

I asked Father Simpson about it first, though. I told him how wrong it felt never to tell my parents anything about my real life here. About my various adventures, about my politics, about Dylan. They had this kind of fantasy vision of me living an abstemious life of prayer and con-templation. They didn't even know I ever left the seminary grounds, that I had any kind of life outside its walls.

Father Simpson laughed uproariously—not the reaction I expected. "Good God," he said. "Don't even go there."

It was like receiving absolution without having to do penance. And I realized that it wasn't just me—that the whole place was a secret from the outside world, that it was "normal" to conceal the truth about our life here. You just had to learn never to talk about how we lived in here, what we did, with anyone on the outside.

Δ

Dear Mom and Dad,

First of all, I want to apologize for not being able to get a letter off for your birthday, Mom. Letters aren't sent out till Sunday, so I guess this will have to do. I sure hope you had a happy Birthday.

We had an Oratory Contest last week, and I did fairly well. I missed by one point getting into the finals. I gave my speech three times, with six other guys. In the first round I was fourth, in the second, I was third, and in the last, first.

Last night we had a party. It lasted for two hours, and we really had a lot of fun. We had two bottles of pop, and handful of cookies, and a dish of ice cream. A lot of guys in humorous gave their speeches, and some of them were really good. By popular request, I was called upon to give mine. Being that the language was somewhat vulgar, they really got a laugh out of it.

Today, the 15th, was the Feast of St. Clement Hofbauer, one of the most famous of Redemptorist Saints. We had a turkey dinner at dinner.

Well, I guess that's about all, so I'll sign off now.

Your Loving Son,
Fred

46

More upsetting was what was happening with little Bob Brodie. He'd started acting strange, losing his temper sometimes in class, getting into fights for no apparent reason. He'd always been a really quiet kid, so this was more than noticeable—it was freakish.

And he started pulling out his hair so much that you couldn't help but notice it. (There turned out to be a name for that: Trichotillomania.)

Mark talked to him one night, far into the night, then came and talked to me. "That poor little guy," he said fondly, "has been sneaking out and going around to stores and shoplifting stuff! He has a ton of it stashed in his locker. He's really screwed up...I don't know what happened to him. He's been doing that stuff for weeks and seems really sad about it. But he can't figure out how to get himself to stop."

My first reaction was to feel jealous that Bob confided like that in Mark instead of me.

47

a symbol

fred williams

    a symbol that has become very prominent in the past few years is the peace action symbol. it has become the standard for many un-american groups who believe, idealistically, in peace. many people here and elsewhere are ignorant of its true meaning or origin.

    it was first used in england on the 21st of february, 1958. the symbol is a composite semaphore signal for the letters "n" and "d," standing for nuclear disarmament. to quote a recent publication on this subject: "it has become a symbol of all who see the military policies of both sides in the cold war as a threat to all men."

    this symbol identifies the person who is wearing it as one who is willing to discuss to try and find alternatives to "our dominantly military foreign policy."

    the symbol is described as follows:

    the central motif: a human being in despair

    the background: eternity

    the circle: the world

    the meaning: a call for practical action on nuclear disarmament.

    there can be no peace except after total nuclear disarmament. a <u>serious</u> attempt must be made soon to negotiate to find peace in southeast asia. it will become a potential target for nuclear weapons in a short while. if you will observe the past two years of the "war" in vietnam you will notice a steady progression from a deadly weapon that will kill 20 soldiers to ones that will kill 100 soldiers (civilians not included, we don't mean to kill them.) soon there will be more powerful weapons. sooner or later one side will suspect the other of installing nuclear missiles. then both sides will have them. a minor nuclear war seems inevitable, a major one probable. we must not force peace by a senseless war.

Δ

Our spring break campout that year was at a place on the Russian River, surrounded by vineyards and apple orchards. Greg McLeod and I took off one day hitchhiking, climbing over fences to pilfer apples when we were hungry. We were wearing what we always wore in those days— Army surplus jackets that we'd bought in Berkeley, with peace action symbols pinned to the lapel—and we stuffed all our pockets full of apples.

Eventually we were picked up by a guy a few years older than we were. Greg offered him an apple, then started pulling them out of all his pockets so the driver could have some choices. "Shit…look at this guy —he's a fuckin' walkin' apple!" the driver said. It made us feel cool—we were passing ourselves off as normal people instead of seminarians.

Δ

One weekend, McLeod and I went off to see *A Thousand Clowns*, with Jason Robards as the main character,

Murray Burns. There was something about his wise-cracking resolute nonconformist act that sent me into a near-frenzy of identification and envy. We stayed and sat through the next showing, as you could in those days, and went back the next weekend and sat through it two more times, by which time I had memorized all of Robards's lines.

I found a hat like his and started wearing it all day long, and tossing off his lines whenever it was even remotely appropriate. For some reason, I felt entitled to equate my life in the seminary with his outside-the-middle-class norm—I'm not sure that I ever came close to working this out intellectually. There just was something about that character that seemed, to me, so "me."

Δ

There was a kid in the class under mine who was another one of those students who struck you as at least partially retarded. Jeff Larsen. He looked kind of like Disney's Goofy—the same teeth, open-mouthed expression, this look like he was always about to say, "yuk-yuk-yuk." He hung around the rec room with McLeod and Vernon and me a lot of the time, and liked to tag along with us whenever we were out walking around. For some reason, he didn't inspire the kind of meanness or hazing that his type usually elicited from the rest of us. We just kind of half-ignored but tolerated him.

One day in the rec room he handed me a folded note and ran out of the room before I could read it. "Happiness is a warm puppy. Fred Moody is a <u>WARM</u> puppy!" Then there was a crude drawing of a floppy-eared little dog.

McLeod was upset. "You have to talk to Father Simpson about this," he said. "This could be something really bad."

It hadn't occurred to me that there was anything all that weird about the note, but now McLeod had me wondering what I was missing. The more he went on about it, the more I felt like something must be wrong with me for not seeing what he saw.

I took it to Father Simpson. He looked at it and asked if Larsen had "ever tried anything." I said no, even though I didn't really know what that "anything" meant. "Well, I wouldn't worry about this," Father Simpson said. "But if he ever tries to feel you up, just let me know."

Δ

It seemed like I'd become extraordinarily dependent on Father Simpson for everything that mattered. His approval meant everything to me. I was certainly closer to him than I was to my family, and I never let a day go by without spending as much time as I could hanging around with him, either in his office or out on the grounds. I felt like I had a connection with him that none of the other seminarians had.

48

That spring seemed largely taken up with a series of long visits from higher-ups in the Redemptorist order. We didn't really notice anything out of the ordinary until about the third or fourth time one of these guys showed up.

They would come out and spend a few days at a time, attending our services, sitting in on our classes, having meetings with groups of seminarians, asking countless questions. It got to be unsettling—like having adults show up all of a sudden at a place where adolescents had been living unsupervised. And it seemed from the tenor of their questions that they were concerned about how lax things were.

Father Simpson was vague about it at first, but after a few weeks he had to let it be known—to some of us, at least—what was going on.

It was a shocker: he said that the Redemptorists were rethinking their seminary program, and that one of the things they were considering was closing Holy Redeemer down.

Δ

I was horrified. Frightened. I couldn't imagine what I would do. My faltering faith aside, there was no way I could go back home and I couldn't imagine transferring to any other seminary. I mean, there was no way any other school was going to let me live the way I was living here.

I felt almost like someone who'd been in hiding, or living as a criminal. Suddenly the secret life was over and once it was out in the open you wondered why on earth you thought you could ever get away with living like that. And particularly why you thought it would never end.

Δ

And then I just decided it couldn't possible happen. We still had some sixty students here, and the Church still needed priests. And it wasn't like the Redemptorists were planning to phase themselves out of business—I mean, they still wanted to educate and ordain new priests for the order.

The more we talked amongst ourselves, the more we found ourselves saying, believing, that in the end they wouldn't do anything that drastic, that everything would be all right, that everything would go on as before.

Δ

More and more, it seemed like religious observance and study was less and less of what we were doing there. We'd be up most of the night, then sleep through classes next day. There was a definite—if unacknowledged—feeling that we were in a kind of freefall, with there being no point in us being serious about our studies or our vocations anymore.

Δ

Mark Reilly and I were up one night and finally went outside at around 3am. We were sitting on the wall at the top of the hill, looking down past the fields at Oakland, just wallowing in our misery. We hardly spoke at all—just sat there feeling incredibly sad, with our sorrow deepening by the minute. There wasn't any explanation for it—we were just overcome by this deep melancholy.

Father Simpson came out...he must have heard us walk out of the building or something.

"What's wrong with you two?"

"I don't know...we just feel shitty."

He sat down on the wall and waited for us to say something more. Minutes went by without us saying a word. And you could tell that he was more and more alarmed the longer we sat there.

"Did something happen?"

"No...we don't really know how to explain it."

"I mean...is it just the blues or something?"

Neither of us could think of an answer.

"Come on," he said, finally. And he led us into his office. He turned on his lights, sat down at his desk, opened a drawer, and pulled out a bottle of Kahlua.

It was a little shocking to think that Father Simpson kept alcohol in his office desk. I'd never tasted alcohol of any kind, and had never seen Kahlua—I still don't know how I recognized it as alcohol, unless it was because of the look on Father Simpson's face. He saw my confusion and said, "It's a coffee liqueur—it'll help you feel better." He pulled out some paper cups from somewhere and poured us all little drinks.

I took a tentative sip, found that it tasted all right, and took a gulp. And felt a wonderful heat immediately suffuse my brain.

Δ

We had probably three drinks or so apiece, by which time I was feeling blissful and a little disoriented. We were talking about all kinds of stuff, just joking around mostly, definitely feeling better, when Father Simpson said, "Let's go down and say Mass together."

Δ

The monastery was deeply quiet. We helped Father Simpson get his vestments on, got out hosts and wine, and went out with him to the main altar. In the middle of the night, to be suddenly bathed in all this light…it was strange. Your basic religious experience. We felt like early Christians, secretly celebrating Mass in the Catacombs, the Romans lurking murderously up above ground.

Mark and I served the Mass. It was without doubt the most deeply spiritual Mass I'd ever experienced—the most deeply spiritual experience of my life, for that matter. It was the first time ever that I felt what could be called the tangible presence of God.

Δ

We finished Communion and gave each other the Kiss of Peace—another post-Vatican II addition to the Mass, where you put your hands on the arms of your partner, leaned forward, and whispered "Peace be with you" or whatever. Mark and I exchanged ours, then each of us in turn did the exchange with Father Simpson.

He put his mouth right next to my ear. "I love you, you fool," he said.

Δ

I was pretty sure he'd said something different to Mark. And I believed there was nothing wrong with what he'd said—that it was Agape, basically, even though I also thought it was something unique to him and me.

I never did know what he'd said when he gave Mark the Kiss of Peace. We never told each other what he'd said to each of us. The closest we came was when we were back up in the dorm, and Mark said, "That was pretty weird what he said there, don't you think?"

I just nodded. I could tell he was trying to get me to go first, before he'd tell me what had been said to him. But I didn't want to talk about it, for some reason—it seemed too private, for reasons I couldn't really explain—and I thought I could tell that Mark didn't either. There was something forbidden-feeling about it.

But I also didn't want either of us to say something that would take away that feeling I was clinging to: that it was basically okay, what Father Simpson said.

49

Things finally got to the point with little Bob Brodie where Father Simpson had to do something. I think he finally got caught shoplifting. Father Simpson called him into his office, and word got around really quickly that this was a Big Deal. Mark and I kept walking past the office and looking in, seeing Brodie sitting there across the desk from Father Simpson, talking and talking and talking. Every time we walked by, he'd be yammering away, and Father Simpson would just be listening.

That evening, Father Simpson called me and Mark in. "You guys—not just you two but a bunch of you upperclassmen—absolutely have got to leave that kid alone. He goes on and on about all these memories, all these good times that are long gone, and they're all stuff he shouldn't even know about. It's all from before he was even here. He's walking around feeling like all these other people's tormenting memories are his. It's enough!"

It was the only time I'd ever seen him at all angry about anything. We were being disciplined—like we were children, students, miscreants, instead of friends.

I said leaving Brodie alone wouldn't be any problem. Which, in truth, it wouldn't—he never seemed to have that much time for me.

But Father Simpson didn't seem interested in my intentions.

"What about you, Mark?"

Mark didn't say anything at first, then mumbled something obedient. He was way more upset about this than I was—another one of those jealous moments for me, facing the fact that not only was Mark much closer to Bob than I was, but that it was noticeable to everyone else.

Brodie ended up leaving anyway, so we didn't have to go out of our way to avoid him after all. And Mark and I never talked about what had happened to him after that, never knew why he left, or even exactly when. His was just another one of those sudden disappearances, basically.

50

It wasn't all that much later that they called us all into Chapel one afternoon, before classes were over, and told us that the seminary was closing down after all—at the end of the year—and that the Redemptorists were working on finding a place to go for those of us who wanted to continue on.

After that, they let us have the afternoon off—we just kind of wandered around in groups, no one saying much of anything.

Δ

in memoriam (an initial reaction)

by fred moody

i know it seems strange but like these savages in "the inheritors" (William Golding) i keep getting a "picture" in my mind. you could call it a dream—if i ever dreamt it— but i don't. it's more like a daydream, and it's weird at times, persistent and bothersome.

when it appears, i'm always standing at the end of the corridor by the library door in the classroom building. the corridor seems almost endless, and i just stand there and look at that big door at the end with the homemade "screen" on it.

this sound fills the hall. it's the sound of the echo of that big door closing. it resounds, never ending, just hanging there from the last time the door was closed. it mixes with the sound of empty silence, to make a mournful, slow, sad sound. there's nobody else. just me and the hall and the sound.

i close my eyes, and i'm out in the turnaround. (the more i write, the more this picture becomes a series of pictures.) the pig is gone. the buildings are there, empty and sad like the hall. it's quiet like death. the buildings just sit there—the broken tiles, the washed-out paint, the cracked window, the uneven blinds, the strange structural, and that same weird echo of the closing of the door.

i walk up through the patio, up through the cloister, not daring to open any more doors. it's a fear of what's inside.

nowhere is there another person. everyone is gone, and there's no race. only a sad echo.

if an outsider would come in, he would look, and he wouldn't hear the echo, he wouldn't hear the empty silence, he wouldn't hear the sadness, he wouldn't see.

he would call me weird, and say that it's beautiful—so peaceful and quiet and restful and novel.

i wouldn't say anything, because i'm like the buildings. some people just can't hear.

so i'd leave.

i picture myself back in the turnaround. i start to walk backwards, up to the sky. i walk backwards right over the horizon, leaving forever, knowing that it's not peaceful and quiet and restful and novel.

it's inert.

and i want the smog to swirl in and swallow it up.

Δ

English III	A
Latin III	D
Algebra 2	C
Civic	B
Biology	C
Sacred Doctrine III	A
Speech II	A

51

Dear Mothers and Dads and guys,

It's dusk here. A giant yellow sun just slipped down behind the mountain called Sleeping Lady over there across the bay. And all is quiet—quiet here in my office. Except for the occasional squealing of a quail down on the field. And I guess it's going to be quiet for awhile.

I said I would write one more letter. I hoped to be able to send you the decision regarding this place—but that has already been taken care of by Father Martucci. I am glad the students had a chance to talk it over with him, and I am glad he sent all of you a letter. Regarding your own decisions about the coming school year, I will leave that to the visitors you will have during the summer. They will, I am sure, be able to answer the questions you still have and help you come to a final decision—those of you that have not already.

As to the summer. We send, as we did last year, no strict rules—only some recommendations. We recommend attending Mass as often as you can and taking part in your parish liturgy as many of you were able to do last year. And some good reading and some private prayer. It doesn't hurt, even in the summer, to sit and think quietly once in awhile.

And we recommend a job—or if you're too young to find a steady job, at least find some odd jobs, and be more than ready to help around the house. You're not a privileged character, and surely you should take this opportunity to repay your family for some of the sacrifices they have made in order to send you here.

And maybe school, if you haven't already had it up to your neck and if you find a course around that you might be interested in—like beekeeping or something.

And finally one of the most valuable parts of summer is being able to meet more people at work and around the neighborhood, and to renew old acquaintances. A priest has to live his life among people, and a seminarian should begin to learn to feel at ease with them, and to begin to love and offer his service. I am sure, if you learned anything this year, you learned how important people are, and how important it is for you to respect and accept and understand them.

Finally, let me say how much I have loved these years of working with these guys. They're great people—all of them. Oh, sure, they're young and they need to be yelled at once in awhile. But I learned much from them, and loved them. And I'll certainly take a lot of memories with me to Paris next year. And one day, please God, I'll have the privilege of knowing them again—as priests, if their vocation points that way, but surely as Catholic men wherever the future takes them.

God love all of you.

Father Simpson

Δ

We had left Holy Redeemer that summer knowing that we'd never be back, and having no idea what was in store for us. News a few weeks later that we would be going to another seminary in California brought a measure of relief even though the place in question—St. Anthony's Seraphic Seminary, in Santa Barbara—was a complete unknown. Staying in California, and out of Bellingham High, was all I cared about.

I remember nothing of that summer, but suspect that I spent it filling out paperwork for the new seminary and hoping that a reasonable number of my friends would be going there as well.

Greg McLeod drove up from Portland one weekend to tell me that he'd be going on to St. Anthony's—an enormous relief. But nearly everyone else opted not to go on.

Δ

I got a call early in July from Neil Davis, another of my friends. He was the middle of three Davis sons at Holy Redeemer—all three kids in that family had started out wanting to be priests. But his older brother quit in his fifth year and now he was dropping out as well. "Take care of my little brother," he said. "He's nervous, but he wants to go on."

Δ

Neil's younger brother—Tom—I mean, on the one hand it was a funny request, asking someone like me to watch over someone like him, even though I was older. Tom was the one seminarian who you thought could go all the way. The rest of us were fuckups of one kind or another, but he always had this serenity about him. Saintliness, really. He never got mad at people, never said so much as a single unkind word about anyone. And you'd see when he was in groups where people started in gossiping about someone else, or throwing insults around, he would just quietly walk away. He was never showy about it or anything—never preachy—just quietly, unostentatiously the soul of kindness. True Christian charity. He was the only one of all of us who actually embodied what it was to be a priest.

He did look like a real kid, though, an Innocent. Your first instinct when you saw him was to feel protective. He had this little round wide-eyed face that looked like it had never seen Evil, or harbored so much as a single dubious thought or urge. He was just a pure, kind soul.

Δ

July 27, 1966
2762 Broadway
Bellingham, Washington

Father Xavier J. Harris, O.F.M.
Saint Anthony's Seminary
Santa Barbara, California:

Dear Father Harris:

My name is Fred Moody and I hope to be joining your senior class this fall. I have filled out the forms as best I could, and am sending my picture along with them.

I am presently employed by the city Park Department, and I am working full time at the cemetery, mowing and trimming. It's a good job, not particularly hard, and it has helped me to somewhat widen my field of acquaintances.

I have been writing a lot of letters to my friends and classmates from H.R.C. (many of whom I may never see again) and have received several letters in return. It does a lot of good to keep in touch, I think.

Of the five book reports, I have completed only one, read one of the other books, and am now starting on a third. I know that this is rather slow, but I have been busy, with my job and all. I will try to have all five written and mailed by the middle of August.

Turning more to my interests, it would be best to begin by saying that my main interest, regarding studies at least, is English Literature, particularly poetry. I hope some-day to major in this subject.

I have an affinity for folk music (Joan Baez, Pete Seeger, Woody Guthrie, Leadbelly, Bob Dylan, and Peter, Paul and Mary) and politically, you might say I tend to be left of center.

I love sports. Almost as much as folk music.

With that, I guess I'll close, looking forward to join-ing you in September.

I remain
Yours sincerely
fred moody

P.S. One thing that the form didn't cover, was that I served as associate editor of the <u>bananafish</u>, a student opinion newspaper that was only mildly successful, due to the fact that the majority of the student body lacked any kind of energy or drive regarding opinion.

fred moody

Δ

2762 Broadway
Bellingham, Washington
August 19, 1966

Dear Father Harris,

Today was my last day at work. I plan to get my things organized for school—clothes, baggage, etc. I have to buy quite a few things yet, and I am going to try to get my trunk shipped by Monday.

I made almost 500 dollars this summer, before I started buying things. I will be able to pay most of my tuition, and my parents can easily pay the rest, I think. I tried to pay for as much of it as possible myself.

I was down at the Palisades last Sunday for our Redemptorist picnic, and I saw Father Ochiltree. I was a little disappointed to hear that they hadn't decided on our Redemptorist Father down there yet, but I suppose it'll work out somehow. I hope so anyway. You never know these days.

I am worried about the changes I'll have to make, but I can hope for the best. I'm certain that I'm not the only one that's worried about this year. I have a problem with Latin, and there will be a lot of different things to get used to.

Anyway, I'll see you in about a week, and be ready to give it a real first class college try.

Sincerely, Fred Moody

LII

"Manly priests bring light and life, brighter and fuller, to mankind, and it is through this ministry to human need that they are themselves redeemed."

—*Cletus F. O'Donnell J.C.D.*

Δ

Because the distance was so much greater, and because I was traveling alone this time, my parents decided I should fly rather than travel by train. We argued over my wardrobe, with my mother insisting that people always "dressed up" to fly, and making me wear a sport coat and slacks—my Sunday Mass uniform.

I flew into Los Angeles, took a bus to a Greyhound station, sat there for hours in the middle of the night, terrified, with my bag tucked under my seat, eventually boarded a bus and rode to Santa Barbara. Once in the little station there, I asked directions and walked to the seminary, there being no one from St. Anthony's at the station to greet me.

Δ

St. Anthony's was huge in comparison with Holy Redeemer. Located on land behind an old Mission church, it was picturesque and traditional. Archetypal—a monastery right out of the history books. Adobe-looking buildings, old mission-style architecture, long covered walkways lined with arches, red tile roofs, vast grounds with statues of

St. Francis and other saints at every turn. Covered, maze-like passages with big iron gates. It looked overwhelming, daunting, vaguely medieval.

And—I feel safe in saying this isn't just memory speaking—terribly joyless. You could feel the gloom as soon as you walked onto the grounds.

Δ

I had barely arrived when I was connected with the trunk I'd shipped. Then I was made to get in line with other newcomers and shuffle forward, one at a time, toward a stern little plump friar in horn-rimmed glasses. Father Mario, the Prefect of Discipline. He had a ferocious smile—intimidating, unfriendly, aggressive—and really meaty lips. I had this immediate notion that he smacked them with tremendous volume when he ate.

And those Franciscans still wore the same habits, those brown hooded robes with the rope for a sash, that they wore back in Assisi, back in the day.

Δ

Father Mario was making us come up to him one at a time and open our luggage so he could go through it and confiscate objectionable stuff. Which we all had in abundance, apparently. There was quite a crowd of upperclassman standing around watching, checking out the newcomers.

I'd never been through anything like that before, but it was obviously the custom here—a warning that life was going to be considerably different under the Franciscans.

And you could tell Father Mario was really enjoying himself, wielding his power.

He had a field day with me, taking away *Catcher in the Rye*, all my Dylan albums—he held up *Blonde on Blonde* for everyone to see what an outrageous sinner I was—and various other books. He had this officious manner about him, too—a way of making you feel publicly humiliated as he showily confiscated all your disgusting contraband.

Δ

That little ritual was highly effective in making clear that we were entering a separate world, cut off from the outside in a way that Holy Redeemer never was. And the Franciscans kept reinforcing the message: We learned, for example, that we were restricted to the grounds except for the occasional group outing, that we were to put our mail in the seminary mailbox unsealed, so that it could be censored, and that all our incoming mail would be delivered to us opened and read by the Fathers.

Δ

Rules of Discipline

Seminarians are to show reverence and obedience to the Reverend Rector, Prefect of Discipline and Professors of the Seminary and also to the Brothers.

They are to observe habitual politeness toward one another, aiming to cultivate that charitable, gentlemanly bearing which bespeaks true culture and refinement, so becoming in a candidate for the holy priesthood. Correct table manners are also to be developed with the same end in view.

They are to observe punctuality in all their exercises, neatness in their appearance, good order with regard to their beds, lockers, desks, etc. They are also expected to show care in the cleanliness of the buildings and the campus.

Silence is to be observed during study periods and in the dormitories. All running, loud talking, shouting and whistling are strictly forbidden in the house.

Any student leaving the dormitory during the night without permission is liable to dismissal. Use of the dormitory toilets for prolonged conversations and gathering will be subject to severe penalties.

No student, without special permission is allowed to enter the enclosure, kitchen, workshops, or workmen's rooms. Permission must be obtained from the Rector or Prefect for the use of construction materials belonging to the Seminary. Outside of specified times, permission is likewise required to visit the dormitories.

Students are held responsible for any damage done to the property of the Institution or of any fellow student. Any such damage must be reported immediately to Fr. Prefect.

No student is permitted to retain money for personal use. All money must be deposited with the Seminary authorities. No advance for clothing, dentistry, stationary, traveling fares, etc., will be made by the Seminary.

Students must write to parents or guardians once a week, namely Saturday evening or Sunday morning during the reading period. All correspondence sent or received by the students must pass through the hand of the Rector or Prefect. Students violating this rule are liable to dismissal.

All magazines, publications, papers, music etc., brought to the Seminary must be submitted for approval.

Δ

Greg McLeod had met and fallen in love with a girl over the summer. He'd also read the material St. Anthony's had sent us over the summer more carefully than I had, and thus already knew about the mail business and was prepared for it. He and his new girlfriend planned for her to sign her letters to him with a boy's name, while he sat in here and tried to figure out whether he still wanted to be a priest.

Δ

It was a depressing shock to get to know my new confreres and see how out of it they were. They were real squares—there's no other way to describe them—completely out of touch with current events, politics, music, everything cool. It was as if they'd been raised in a bubble from birth, and wanted to stay in it at all costs. Where at Holy Redeemer we had been going out all the time—to Berkeley, to San Francisco, to demonstrations and rallies—they were effectively cloistered.

Δ

I had only been there a few days before I could feel the scrutiny of the friars, who suspected that I was bent on being disruptive.

Which I was. Not so much because I wanted to enlighten the benighted, though. It was more that I wanted to be seen as hipper than thou.

Δ

My bed was in a vast dorm—no more rooms, even for seniors. There were three times as many students at St. Anthony's as there had been at Holy Redeemer, and the room—even though it housed only third- and fourth-year guys—seemed gigantic. I unpacked and fought off depression by sternly reminding myself that I only needed to stick out one year here—that it would be safe to leave once I'd graduated from high school. I had decided not to envision anything beyond that.

Even so, I couldn't help but feel that I'd made a colossal mistake in coming to this place.

LIII

The Franciscans were careful to keep their Redemptorist newcomers apart from one another as much as possible. Our assigned beds were widely scattered throughout the dorm, which was patrolled nightly by Father Mario; as few of us as possible were assigned to the same sports teams; we were assigned widely separated pews in chapel; and we were made to sit in scattered desks in study hall and class.

Δ

The place was run by Father Xavier Harris, the rector, who cultivated an air of gentleness. He came across at first as the good cop counterpart to Father Mario's bad cop. He was soft-spoken, patient, with gray hair at his temples. Avuncular, kindly.

He really loved being perceived as kindly. Which made for quite a challenge, getting him to lose his temper, although I eventually developed some pretty impressive skills in that regard.

Δ

Father Mario kept coming around, oozing solicitude. There was something about him that made me distrustful, even scared. I never could figure out what the problem was—just that he gave me the creeps. A couple weeks into the year, he started taking me aside between classes, or after chapel or meals, to give me this searching look and ask if there were any problems or concerns I wanted to share with him. I kept telling him no, no, no, until he finally backed off. But I couldn't help noticing how close he seemed to a lot of the guys there. Like I'd been with Father Simpson.

I just couldn't figure it out. He didn't have an ounce of charisma, as far as I could tell. It was really puzzling to see the Franciscan seminarians admiring him so much.

Δ

Father Mario was particularly solicitous of this one kid, a junior nicknamed Barbie. He was plump, fastidious, theatrical, with shiny skin, the most varied wardrobe I've ever seen, and extravagantly effeminate manners. He was really aggressive about acting and talking like a woman… I'd never met anyone like that before, and had no idea what to make of it. We'd always had effeminate guys in the seminary—I particularly remember one confrere a couple years ahead of me at Holy Redeemer known to everyone as Mother—but I'd never seen anyone who was so theatrical about it, like he was doing everything he could to call attention to his girliness.

He was really likable, too. Hilarious. Always on. But he was essentially a female impersonator in male clothing. And he loved his nickname—it was his whole identity, really—certainly more so than his given name, or his seminarianness.

You couldn't imagine him as a priest—he was too irreverent about convention, for one thing; and so aggressively feminine in his dress, demeanor, behavior, that he

Fred Moody

seemed always to be performing. Trying to picture him in a Franciscan habit, all calmed down and serious, "priestly"— you just couldn't get that to happen.

Δ

My own aggressive nonconformity was confined to constant rants at my new confreres about the rules, the restrictions, the backwardness of this place, and never taking off my Jason Robards/Murray Burns hat except in chapel and when we went to bed at night.

Δ

It's hard to tell, from this remove, how reliable my memory about Father Mario is, how dubious about him I really was at the time. But ever since I found out what he had been doing to kids there, I've had this conviction that his early approaches to me were like those of a shark bumping or rubbing against creatures in an effort to assess their foodworthiness. And reports that came out recently about him confirm that remembered impression. "As St. Anthony's Prefect of Discipline, Fr. Mario Cimmarrusti employed numerous schemes and pretenses, and utilized his status as an authority figure, to allow him to groom and assault St. Anthony's students. His first step was to 'screen' the student to see if that student was susceptible to abuse. The screening process involved Fr. Cimmarrusti fondling the student; if the student became aroused and embarrassed, Fr. Cimmarrusti used this against the student to force his silence as the abuse continued. If the student did not become aroused, Cimmarrusti was less likely to sexually abuse that student further."

I think there was an additional, more preliminary

element to that screening—that his sniffing around me let him know that I was unlikely to keep my mouth shut if he proceeded to the next item on the screening agenda.

Δ

It's virtually impossible now to make people understand how benighted we were about sexual matters back then. How infinitely susceptible to abuse we were by virtue of our innocence—our ignorance. We lacked the imagination, the information, to make sense of the abuse clues constantly being thrown at us. And for all of my remembered reaction to Father Mario, I never had any specific suspicion about him. I just got a vibe from him that I didn't like—I never could figure out what it was that set off those little alarms.

Δ

Even though…I mean, you could actually witness things and have no idea what you were seeing. It was a form of blindness—I can't think of any other way to describe it. Your brain simply could not interpret what your eyes and ears were taking in.

St. Anthony's was built on top of a bluff looking down into a deep, dramatic canyon. Really steep—this breathtaking view over all these trees and shrubs growing out of cliff-steep hillsides. The shrubs were mostly poison oak—a dangerous plant that had no equivalent in the Northwest. We'd had lots of poison oak at Holy Redeemer, too, but for some reason kids from the Pacific Northwest had an immunity to it.

At first. Invariably, the immunity went away after a few years, and I was at St. Anthony's only a few weeks when I came down with a horrible case of poison oak—massive skin rash, an excruciating itch, swelling all over, with my eyes nearly swollen shut and an oozing, golden crust all over my skin.

There wasn't much you could do by way of treatment. You just had to wait it out by lying naked in a bed under a canopy that held the covers up so as to keep them from touching your skin. And you had to do everything in your power not to scratch, since you'd end up lacerating yourself and spreading the poison to other parts of your body with your contaminated hands.

So there I was in the infirmary—this ten-bed little cabin behind the dorm, overlooking the canyon—with a Franciscan sophomore named Gordy Lester, who had a high fever. We'd been talking off and on but stopped as soon as we heard the door open.

It was Father Mario—it's funny how you could tell it was him, how the way his rosary clicked when he walked around was immediately recognizable as his sound alone.

We were the only two guys in there on this particular night. I was burrowed down in my bed, under that canopy, and figured out later that Father Mario didn't know I was there.

He came in and went right over to Gordy's bed. "How are you feeling?" he asked. Very concerned—not the way he talked to people during the day, when he was playing disciplinarian rather than doctor.

I couldn't hear what Gordy said…just this low mumble.

"Well, I'm afraid this looks pretty serious," Father Mario said. "You're really feverish, and fevers can be dangerous; we're going to have to try to bring your temperature down. The first thing I'll have to try is an alcohol rubdown."

I could hear him go over to some cabinets on the wall and get something, then come back to Gordie's bed. Then I heard a little rustling. Then Father Mario said, "Let's just get you out of these pajamas now, OK?" Then just this really long silence during which all I could hear was Father Mario breathing, Gordy's bedsprings squeaking a little…and you could definitely sense serious weirdness.

I was really tuned in. I could tell something was profoundly wrong with what was going on over there, but I had no idea what. So mostly I just lay there thinking about how I was hearing "the sounds of silence," like in the Simon & Garfunkel song. How silence like that is the kind where you can actually feel it trying to tell you something.

Father Mario left after fifteen minutes or so. I heard the door close and waited for another few minutes for Gordy to say something. But he was utterly silent—another silence you could hear, like it had deep meaning.

I mean, I could tell he was really upset.

"Gordy? Are you all right?"

"…."

"Gordy?"

Fred Moody

"...."

It was maybe an hour later when he started up our conversation again, all normal and everything. Not a word about Father Mario. And neither one of us ever mentioned that visit—we just put it out of our minds.

Δ

It took me forty-three years after leaving that place to try to track down any of my confreres. I managed to find Gordy through an alums' web site, and emailed him.

Since I hadn't really known him and had never talked with him much except for that time we spent in the infirmary, I was surprised at first that he remembered me. But then I realized he remembered me only because I'd been there with him during one of the worst nights of his life.

Δ

We exchanged some email before I got around to asking him about that night. His answer:

I was in the infirmary with the flu, so "doctor" Cimmarrusti gave me an alcohol rub down, purportedly to take down the fever. I realized afterward that he had gotten some sort of jollies out of it. I was already on the defensive for having been caught sneaking some food into the infirmary.

How was your St. Anthony's experience? I would guess that coming in as a senior Mario would have left you alone. I certainly hope so. I've gotten pieces of the history after I left, but of course I get one bit at one time and another bit at another time, so my picture isn't very clear. I heard there was some big blow-up centered on Tony Giles (I hope I'm remembering his name right) whom I remember as a pretty good guy. I recently got together with Jeff Almquist, Mike Hahn, and Jack Rhoads at an event for survivors. There's a follow up on 10/16, where the San Francisco archbishop and his auxiliary will meet with the survivors, which I plan to attend with Jeff, Mike and Jack.

LIV

I took an immediate dislike to everything about
St. Anthony's except the weather. The strict discipline was
disgusting, most particularly the censorship. I started complaining constantly, inside and outside of class. Refusing
to study Latin, making grandiose speeches to my confreres
about its irrelevancy. Showily not participating in prayer
and Mass—just going through the motions silently. Arguing in Sacred Doctrine class against everything from taking
the Bible literally to celibacy.

I'm not sure why I started speaking out against
celibacy, since it was more or less my primary reason for
having entered the seminary. And I had come to see it not
as a blessing, a way of avoiding girls, so much as a curse I
would have to live with anyway, because girls would always
be determined to avoid me.

But then again, I was arguing against everything at
the time, trying to piss off the Fathers as much as I could.

I hadn't been an ideal student at Holy Redeemer,
but I had respected the Fathers there, for the most part. But
these friars—I just thought they were a joke.

Δ

The argument for celibacy always went back to
the New Testament stories about the Apostles, citing the
fact that St. John, the only unmarried Apostle, was "Jesus's favorite." Father Harris, who taught Sacred Doctrine,

brought that up during one of our arguments in class, and I blurted out—thinking about how John was always depicted in paintings—"He wasn't Jesus' favorite because he was unmarried! It was because he was so soft and fine!" I heard McLeod in the back of the room snickering, but no one else got the Don Kalvin reference.

Father Xavier may not have gotten the reference, but he got the meaning, and he was furious—an unexpected bonus. Normally, he seemed to relish our exchanges, but this time his face turned instantly red—a definite loss of control. It was highly entertaining to see him lose his phony *gravitas* like that.

He got himself back under control almost immediately, then brought down the first of what became a regular punishment for me—banishment to a little empty room at the top of the seminary tower during all of our recreation periods, for a week. I spent the time trying to learn the guitar.

Δ

McLeod was feeling more and more fearful about his correspondence with his disguised girlfriend. He wanted to say more in his letters, be more romantic, but he didn't dare.

I finally told him that I'd start taking them off the grounds to an outside mailbox in the middle of the night.

And then came something surprising. Once word got around about what I was doing, all these Franciscan students—people I thought were so compliant, so cowed—

started coming up and asking if I'd deliver mail for them, too. Which of course I was only too happy to do.

I started calling it my "Midnight Mail Service"—a weekly mission that turned near-daily within a few weeks, due to heavy demand. I'd wait until three or so in the morning, quietly get out of bed, dress, and sneak out the back door by the canyon. Terrified of being caught. Wildly excited.

The walk down the long road out of the grounds in the deep warm southern California dark, with the scent of all these exotic desert flowers in the air, the deep deep silence, and the terrible thrilling fear of capture—I've never forgotten the absolute joy of those walks.

LV

The St. Anthony's counterpart to *The Coast-line* was
The Antonian:

the antonian

a literary magazine

published quarterly by the students of

saint Anthony seminary

high school

To stimulate the questing mind to reach for truth;

To direct the searching spirit to pursue goodness;

To harness the creative energies to formulate beauty—

These are the goals of literary art,

These are the goals of the Antonian.

As St. Francis composed his Canticle of the Sun

And St. Anthony his Sermons on the Word of God,

So their modern counterparts

Here express their deepest sentiments.

Father Xavier Harris, O.F.M., Rector

Δ

Every day that fall and winter I stepped outside to spectacular weather—a never-ending miracle. I never managed to get used to it. The incongruity between that heavenly ambience and the hellish institution plunked down in it was constantly on my mind. To be trapped in such a miserable place set in such a paradise…it was crazy-making torture.

Δ

In spite of our inability and refusal to fit in, the Franciscans had us participating fully in student life on the theory that we'd eventually acclimatize. For seniors, this included a monthly turn at delivering a homily to the student body at morning meditation. The procedure called for the senior in question to write up his homily and turn it in to the Fathers for approval the day before.

On my first try, I turned in a homily on Zen Buddhism. Less out of any real understanding or appreciation of Zen than a desire to provoke a reaction.

In that, I was a little disappointed; it was early in the year and the Fathers hadn't given up on me yet, so they reacted with a degree of indulgence. I got my submission back with a note on it: "You can deliver this one, but from now on, stick to Christian sources."

Δ

The dorms were laid out on one huge floor, in an H configuration, with one room being for the two upper classes, the other for the freshmen and sophomores. In between were the showers, on each side of which were narrow hallways lined with sinks and mirrors on both walls. Those halls were maddening—the facing mirrors gave you an infinite series of reflections that seemed to hint at something magical, heretical. I would stand there staring down this cascade of diminishing selves, trying to find the last one. The idea that they went on forever was intolerable, impossible, fascinating. And I had this irrational sense that there was a forbidden message in this experience.

Δ

I was standing alone after a flag football game one Saturday afternoon, between the mirrors, peering into the abyss, when another figure/series suddenly materialized: Father Mario.

Up went my hackles.

He had a way of suddenly showing up like that wherever you were, without having made a sound. Which was odd, given that he was all but defined by the sound his rosary made when he patrolled the dorm at night, or walked up and down the aisles between rows of desks during study hall. I noticed in both cases that eventually he would stop beside someone's desk, or bed, pretty much every night, tap him on the shoulder, and take him off to his office.

Study hall was particularly weird that way: He would take a student off to his office, that student would come back a half hour or so later and silently tap the desk of another, who would go off to Father Mario's office, that student would eventually come back and tap the next one's desk…it generally went on like that every night at study hall, the same series of guys getting special counseling.

Δ

REDEMPTORIST SEMINARIANS JOIN ST. ANTHONY'S STUDENT BODY

Twenty-five Redemptorist seminarians have joined the St. Anthony's seminary student body. The move from their former campus, Holy Redeemer Seminary, in Oakland, California, came when the priests of the Redemptorist province found that operation of the seminary was no longer feasible. The seminary was closed with the permission of the Redemptorist Superior General in Rome.

A number of Redemptorist priests were sent out to visit various seminaries, with the aim of finding one that would be similar to Holy Redeemer in spirit, and willing to incorporate the Redemptorist seminarians into the student body. After careful consideration St. Anthony's Seminary was chosen because of its location and because the spirit prevalent here was not found to be notably different from that of the former Holy Redeemer Seminary.

Δ

It took me all of a week at St. Anthony's to wish I could track down the moron who decided the "spirit" in this hellhole "was not found to be notably different" from the paradise they'd closed down.

LVI

I sent a letter through the normal St. Anthony's mail to Vernon, in which I complained that I'd landed in the "fourteenth century," and went on to detail all the backwardness I had to contend with, all the rules, all the outdated notions.

The day after I sent the letter, Father Mario went through his announcements at lunch, as he did every day, then delivered an aside: "I know it can seem like the fourteenth century here…." He shot me a quick glance—just enough to let me know that he'd read, and registered, what I'd written.

Δ

The routine at St. Anthony's—an unvarying, stultifying, soul-killing schedule of prayer, study, organized sports, and meals—was broken up in October by a massive forest fire in the canyons and hills around the seminary. At one point, we were told to prepare to evacuate the place. We could see raging fires on the other side of the canyon and there was a pretty good chance that they would leap over to our side and come roaring up the slopes to the seminary grounds.

I spent every free moment at the little low wall over the canyon, looking out at the spectacle, which was Biblical in scale. It went on for days, the seminary wreathed in thick smoke. I'd never seen anything like it. The Californians, though, took it all in stride.

Δ

The only other excitement those first few months—
aside from my Midnight Mail Service outings—came when
the Fathers announced at lunch one day that we would
be putting on *A Thousand Clowns* for our annual theatrical
performance, and that we should sign up for auditions.

I felt that Fate was coming round at last—that there
might be a reason for me to be at St. Anthony's after all.
And the more I thought about it, the more I was convinced
that the play was meant to be, that I was meant to play
Murray Burns. Even the news that the cast would include
girls from a nearby Catholic girls' school—and that if I got
the Murray Burns part I'd have to kiss one of them—didn't
sway me.

Δ

Only one other seminarian—a popular senior
named Joe Mallahan—signed up to audition for the Murray Burns part. We were given the script for the single scene
we'd be reading, but given Mallahan's popularity, I wasn't
taking any chances: I memorized all the Murray Burns lines
in the play—I all but had them memorized anyway, from
repeated viewings of the movie—and made Greg McLeod
help me rehearse them. Day after day, we'd spend our free
periods in an empty classroom, with me delivering lines,
refining the part, perfecting the act from beginning to end.
Seeing alternately myself as Murray Burns, the consummate rebel, nonconformist, and Murray Burns as me, driving the seminary overlords insane with my irreverent antics,
my refusal to give in, my cute and clever ways of constantly
frustrating them.

Δ

McLeod may have been willing to put in all this time because he'd completely lost interest in everything else at St. Anthony's. All he cared about anymore was his new girlfriend, to whom he was writing every day. I was making deliveries for him four or five times a week now, and on some of those nights I'd be carrying twenty or more letters as my roster of clients kept growing.

I was coming back from a delivery one night when one of the Fathers happened to be out. When he confronted me, I told him I'd just been feeling sad and wanted to go for a walk. He'd seen me come in through the gate, though, so he knew I'd been off the grounds.

I had to meet with Father Mario and Father Harris, and this time was sent off to the tower for three weeks. During which time I had to do my audition rehearsing on my own.

Δ

I wasn't the only one among the Redemptorists having trouble fitting in. We were all unhappy—shocked, even—at the repressive and joyless atmosphere of the place. Three of my classmates had dropped out by the end of October, and it was clear that McLeod wasn't going to last much longer. He may have been the only one there whose grades were dropping faster than mine.

And Tom Davis, two years younger, who'd been more or less left in my care by his older brother, was clearly depressed. He was looking horrible—you could tell he wasn't sleeping properly—and terribly sad all the time. He withdrew from the community entirely, spending all his free time alone. He was never interested in doing anything with anyone else—he just tried to disappear, basically. A self-imposed internal exile.

I tried to talk to him about it, but he just shrugged me off.

I felt bad, because of my promise to his brother, but there didn't seem any way for me to get through to him, to find out what was wrong.

Not that I didn't understand—I mean, it wasn't exactly a mystery. Anyone in his right mind would have been depressed by this place. I was pretty sure he was basically suffering from the same thing I was: shock, depression, the hopeless feeling that his dream was dying and he had nowhere else to go.

Δ

It wasn't just that you couldn't endure public high school. Worse was facing your devout Catholic family. To go home a failure after all the hopes and dreams they'd invested in you, to bring shame down on your family in the eyes of the other parishioners…it was horrifying even to imagine. Particularly in a family like mine, where no one had any idea I was unhappy, troubled, no longer believing I had a vocation. For all they knew, I was living a happy life of prayer and contemplation. Any time I pictured the shock there if I told my parents what was really going on, that I wanted to come home, I would immediately shut that option off in my mind.

LVII

Here's what passed for excitement at St. Anthony's.

Seminarians and Fathers alike there were in a constant defensive posture—against nonbelievers, against liberal Catholics, against atheists…. So one of the biggest bombshells to hit the place was the April 1966 issue of *Time* magazine, its cover a big black rectangle with the magazine name at the top and down below, in red, the words, "Is God Dead?" Inside, the writers intoned: "Is God dead? The three words represent a summons to reflect on the meaning of existence. No longer is the question the taunting jest of skeptics for whom unbelief is the test of wisdom and for whom Nietzsche is the prophet who gave the right answer a century ago. Even within Christianity, now confidently renewing itself in spirit as well as form, a small band of radical theologians has seriously argued that the churches must accept the fact of God's death, and get along without him."

Δ

Months later, the cover story was still wreaking havoc at St. Anthony's. The question was seen as a dangerous assault, something that had to be rebutted, squelched, stopped in its tracks. And the Church did indeed strike back that fall, with a special broadcast by the country's most famous archbishop, Fulton J. Sheen.

Archbishop Sheen was revered in the American Catholic Church for having readily adopted a new medium—television—for powerful and effective preaching. He was a master at high-impact TV presentations with dramatic lighting, lots of moving around, and various histrionics that would have looked silly in real life.

They actually looked pretty silly to me on television, but the general Catholic population seemed to love his act.

So his coming special broadcast rebuttal to the God is Dead movement was big news at St. Anthony's. People talked about it for weeks ahead of time, and when the night of the broadcast finally came, it was treated like a holiday. People counted down to it all day long, we were given the evening off from Study Hall so we could watch it, and the Fathers set up a television in the refectory so the whole student body could crowd in and take it in together.

Greg McLeod and I sat together in the back of the room, snickering and making secret little snide comments at all the ridiculous poses Sheen kept striking. He walked around in this big cape, like God's vampire, turning around theatrically again and again, his cape flying, to confront the camera.

And then he got to the climax, the payoff. "Does all this convince me that God is Dead?" he asked. Dramatic pause. "No...but it does convince me that *Satan is very much alive!*"

McLeod and I howled with derision. We were thoroughly drowned out, protected, by the cheering of everyone else, which served to further fuel our self-righteousness.

Δ

The last letter I delivered via my Midnight Mail Service for McLeod was the letter to his girlfriend telling her that he was coming home for good. He managed to last for only three months in this place, and most of that time he'd spent wondering why he'd come.

It was what he had to do, I knew, but it sent me into a tailspin anyway. McLeod was the only person keeping me even remotely sane.

Then it hit me that what had been feeling like an eternity of misery had in fact been only a few weeks. And now it was going to get a lot worse; with my last real con-frere leaving, I'd be entirely alone—no more fellow-suffer-ers.

And I knew that I really couldn't keep putting off the same questions McLeod finally had the guts to face: about myself, my future, my lies.

Δ

I threw myself all the more furiously into my *Thousand Clowns* rehearsals, getting ready for the audition scheduled for right after Christmas break. I was careful to let it be known to everyone how hard I was working on this, how much more work than necessary I was doing—all to make sure that the director, Pete Lowry, would know better than to deny me.

Δ

I was walking from the study hall across the parking lot to the dorm one afternoon when I came upon a group of seminarians standing outside the Fathers' quarters. It turned out they were standing under Father Mario's open office window, on the second floor.

Everyone was freaked out. And I could hear horrible screams coming from that window—Barbie's voice.

We all stood there looking at each other, wondering what was going on. Incredibly confused. There just wasn't anything normal about those sounds. Even the Franciscan upperclassmen, long familiar with the place, were looking panicky.

We couldn't figure out how much we should be troubled, whether what we were hearing was weird, bad, whether we should be telling somebody about it. But mostly we were just wanting it to be over.

We all knew that Father Mario had a special interest in Barbie, and that the two of them were close. Which made this all the more upsetting. None of us knew what to do, whether we were even supposed to be noticing. In fact, it occurred to me that we could get in trouble if we were caught noticing like this, eavesdropping.

We couldn't imagine what was going on up there, what Barbie had done to deserve that level of punishment, what Father Mario was doing to make him scream like that.

And not one of us, as far as I know, ever told or asked Father Harris or any of the other Fathers about it.

Δ

It made me think later about how trapped we were, how isolated. (Why it took me so long to understand this,

I'll never understand.) And how we could even be stuck in here with a murderer and never be able to get anyone on the outside to believe it. Catholic priests were revered figures—I couldn't imagine getting either of my parents to believe anything bad about anyone in the clergy. To give voice to the kind of unease I felt around Father Mario would be to invite opprobrium, even punishment, from my parents.

That's the way it was for all of us—even if we wanted to tell the truth about the Fathers, we couldn't.

Δ

THE KING SPEAKS

Tom Davis

On my chessboard
　　　I am the king.

I have no troubles
　　　That my friends
　　　Will not take care
　　　Of for Me.

They shall do
　　　What I say
　　　Or shall be left
　　　By the wayside.

My bishops and knights
　　　In my kingdom
　　　Are wealthy all,
　　　Because of Me.

But I am wealthier
    Than they;
    If they try
    To overtake
    Me,
    I shall make
    Them outcasts.

Nobody shall be greater
    Than me.

My pawns—ah yes,
    My pawns.

They do not bother
    Me;
    I shall use them
    When needed;
    But when I
    Am finished with them—
    Ah,
    They are but a pebble
    On an ocean beach.

Tom Davis—Tom comes to us as a Redemptorist seminarian from Whittier, California. Here is a guy that writes poetry with soul. It is no wonder that he likes music, especially that of Joan Baez.

Δ

English IV	B
Latin IV	D
Spanish I	B
Social Science	B
Physics	C
Sacred Doctrine IV	A
Art Appreciation	B
Religious Exercises	D
Authority	D
Studies and Work	C
Fellow Students	C
Responsiveness	D
Reliability	B
Courtesy	C
Neatness	C

LVIII

Nov. 20, 1966

Dear Father Xavier,

We were a little dismayed when we received Fred's grades, particularly his personality evaluation.

We would appreciate it if you could drop us a note and give us your impressions as to what is occurring.

From his past academic record, you have probably noted his excellent grades in religion and deportment. To have this happen in his senior year is upsetting to us, as you can undoubtedly imagine.

As we are so far away and find a personal visit impossible at this time, we would greatly appreciate a word from you.

Our prayers are with all of you.

Sincerely,

Anna M. Moody

Δ

November 24, 1966

Dear Mrs. Moody,

Thank you for writing us about Fred. We were in hopes that
he would report back to you the faculty evaluation which
I took great pains to spell out to him and which was explained to him by Father Ochiltree in a counseling session.

To quote Father Mario, our prefect, Fred is a disciplinarian's
night-mare. He is, and this is no exaggeration, the most
non-observant seminarian we have ever encountered at St.
Anthony's. Because Fred came to us as a senior from another seminary we have been extraordinarily tolerant of his
"deviant" behavior and his non-conformist mentality. We
have also given him credit for good will and non-malicious
intent. However, at times, Fred's behavior has been so deviant that we had to call him to account. I will briefly indicate
some of these incidents which are only typical of countless
others for which he has not been called to answer.

The first of these events took place when Fred arose one
night at 3:00 a.m., awakened another seminarian and asked
him to go for a walk. The student prefect was awakened
by the disturbance and the proposed walk was summarily
cancelled as Fred, without bothering to identify himself,
disappeared into the night.

Sometime later, Fred, disturbed by Greg McLeod's decision
to leave the seminary, became dejected, absented himself
from exercises, left dinner early and failed to participate in
his class' Halloween entertainment.

Despite his considerable ability, which we readily recognized, Fred has refused to study Latin because he fails to see its immediate value. Fred consistently fails to genuflect when he enters chapel; until recently did not join in public prayers or song; paid little or no attention to prayers in refectory, and generally gave such a poor example of external piety that he was a scandal to his fellow seminarians.

I say scandal deliberately because Fred is tremendously admired and sedulously imitated by many seminarians, both Redemptorist and Franciscan. Fred makes what appears to be a studied effort to be different from others. He possesses an attractive personality and a genuine interest in his fellow seminarians and hence exercises considerable influence over them. His unacceptable behavior is all the more a problem.

Fred was marked down in courtesy because he insisted on wearing a hat during study hall and failed repeatedly to excuse himself when he came late for exercises. He was marked down in neatness because his bed and locker were found to be in a bad state of disarray.

With this brief account of some of Fred's activities you must think that we have given up on him. Far from it. We recognize a great deal of potential in Fred. I teach him in two classes, sacred doctrine and social science, and find him an interested student and extremely perceptive. At first he had an almost uncontrollable urge to talk out in class and at almost any other time he felt like it. He has moderated this urge and is now a pleasure to have in class. Some of Fred's unconventionality is charming and refreshing. He takes new slants on things and possesses an originality that is stimulating. But he has made a cult of non-conformity and dares anyone to criticize him for being "himself." It is this please [sic] of sincerity which Fred expects to end all arguments and to win all debates. Perhaps another school or another seminary might accept Fred's version of himself, but we find it opposed to the ideal of the priesthood which we are trying to develop in the students who are committed to our care.

In all of our many differences with Fred we have stressed the fact that it is his responsibility to accept our way of doing things even though he may not always agree. Instead, he has expected us to make rather extravagant allowances for his peculiar way of thinking and acting. When corrected he has not been obstinate or perverse but he has been very slow to change and has usually had recourse to some new way of asserting his differences.

Father Mario and I have both recognized a great deal of good in Fred and in his philosophy. It is our opinion that he has carried some good things too far and that he has become so wrapped up in his efforts to be a non-conformist and so enamoured of his personal ideals that he cannot accept a community form of life and work. Unless he changes radically and gives some evidence soon, we must judge him unfit for the religious life and for the priesthood. There are other fields where Fred's bent for non-conformity may not be a handicap, e.g. acting, journalism, folk singing. But even the most tolerant seminary will find him, if not a nightmare, at least a severe headache.

Since I talked to Fred after the first quarter reports, I feel that he has made a greater effort to conform with the standards and procedures of St. Anthony's. If he continues in this effort he will be welcome to return after Christmas.

Perhaps during the Christmas holidays you will have an opportunity to discuss these evaluations at greater length and in more detail. It may be that we are too demanding or that our standards are too strict. As a former principal of two high schools for a period of twelve years, I must say that a boy like Fred would have been a problem for me even in the more permissive atmosphere of a diocesan high school.

Because the Redemptorist Fathers and ourselves are working very closely together, I am asking Father Ochiltree to read my letter to you and to add any comments of his own he might wish to make. We are very much aware and have been from the beginning that St. Anthony's and Holy Redeemer of last year, are operated in a very different manner. We have made full allowance for this fact. Even after this allowance, we are convinced that Fred, up until now, has not acted in a manner becoming of a seminarian.

If this letter of mine causes you concern and you would prefer to speak directly with me over the telephone, please feel free to call me. Let me know by post card when to expect your call. I will see that Fred is in the office with me and we can, hopefully, come to a better understanding.

Thank you again for your letter and be assured of our sincere interest to help your son attain his goal.

> Sincerely in Christ,
> Xavier J. Harris, O.F.M.
> Rector

Δ

Fred Moody
Official Court Reporter
Court House
Bellingham, Washington 98225

November 28, 1966

Father Xavier J. Harris, OFM, Rector

Saint Anthony's Seminary
Garden and Pueblo Streets
Santa Barbara, California

Dear Father:

Thank you very much for your letter of November 24th
to Mrs. Moody in answer to her inquiry regarding Fred's
grades in conduct.

Fred had reported to us following his faculty evaluation that
he was having some problems and had been placed on probation. However, we certainly did not realize the problem
had reached the degree it obviously has, and we are both
most disturbed and disappointed. We have not, of course,
heard from either the Franciscans or the Redemptorists
since Fred has been there this year, and our only indica-
tion of his problem was through his letters to us, in which
he mentioned from time to time that he was having some
difficulty.

This is one of the disadvantages of being so far away. However, at this particular time it might be a blessing for all
concerned that I am up here where I can't get my hands on
him. I think I would be sorely tempted to remove his hat

with a length of lead pipe, for a starter, and then to take whatever other steps were necessary to bring him into line.

I certainly think you have been more than patient with Fred, much more so than I would be. It certainly appears to me at this stage of the game that he is completely lacking in the qualifications needed to become a priest, and although it is, of course, our hope that he does stick it out, I certainly am going to take a long look at the situation when he comes home for Christmas, and if he is fortunate enough to be allowed to return, I will take a much longer and deeper look into the situation next summer.

Thank you again for your long and detailed letter. Please keep us advised of his progress, and if there is anything you feel would be beneficial from this end, please let us know. You may feel free to show Fred this letter if you wish.

Sincerely
Fred Moody

Δ

I came home for Christmas in a massive funk. I had no idea that my parents and Father Harris had been exchanging letters, and my parents—I thought—had no idea I was so troubled, in so much trouble. For all of my dad's promises to Father Harris, neither he nor my mom said a word to me about their correspondence. And I didn't say a word to them about much of anything.

LVIX

I returned from Christmas break to the auditions for *A Thousand Clowns*. Mallahan and I did our scene in front of Carlson, who waited all of a minute or so after we finished to tell me that he'd picked Mallahan.

I sat there, numb, staring into yet another abyss, disbelieving, while he perfunctorily ran through his list of reasons, at the end of which he said, "I mean, you have to be able to kiss a girl in this play and everything."

Δ

It might have been the same day, maybe a day or two later, late at night, when I was sitting in a dark corner of the chapel, brooding. It was by far the most depressed I'd ever been. My self-pity was out of control. I just sat there wallowing, alone, invisible, despairing. I couldn't think of anything in my life to be anything other than deeply depressed about.

It was a Wednesday—the night for Confession. I watched the last of the seminarians come out of the confessional and go up to the altar rail to kneel and do his penance. And I saw the door to the priest's compartment open and Father Mario emerge.

It enraged me, seeing him in the role of confessor. I had no idea why—it just sent me into a ferocious internal frenzy.

Δ

We found out at lunch next morning that Tom Davis had disappeared. He'd been at Mass that morning, but no one had seen him since, and the Fathers decided that he must have left the grounds. By the end of the day, they had contacted the police.

This was a big deal, having a seminarian just mysteriously disappear. Nothing like it had ever happened before in the history of St. Anthony's, as far as anyone knew. The Fathers were visibly panicked.

We heard a couple days later that Tom had been seen at the Santa Barbara airport, and that he had apparently gotten on a plane to Los Angeles.

About a week later, he turned up in Hawaii, of all places, penniless, shoeless, homeless. The police picked him up for vagrancy or something and he told them who he was and where he lived—that is, where his parents lived—but never did tell anyone what on earth he was doing, or why. The police said that he'd picked up a discarded boarding pass and used it to con his way onto a series of airplanes.

We were amazed when we heard all this. Awestruck. How cool is it to con your way all the way to Hawaii? It was way beyond what any of us in this place could imagine even trying.

But I was also freaked out. I mean, there were some people at St. Anthony's who you might be able to imagine trying something like this, but Tom wasn't one of them. It was so out of character that it was scary—he had to have had some kind of breakdown, something really bad, to go off like he did.

Δ

The Davis thing was yet another eye-opener about what a House of Horrors I'd landed in. A part of me was envious of Tom, and sorry that he hadn't somehow been able to just settle down in Hawaii and start a new life as someone else—someone with no memories of this place, no need to explain this part of his life.

Δ

We never heard a word from anyone about why he'd taken off, either. I heard from Neil—who wrote asking me if I knew anything—that Tom never told anyone why he'd fled the seminary and been afraid to go home. I kind of felt like I thought I knew, but I couldn't figure out how to explain it.

LX

The time came round again for me to deliver the homily at morning meditation. I sat there all evening long two nights before, trying to come up with something acceptable to the Fathers that I could stand to deliver. It was a matter of integrity.

I finally wrote a harmless little homily on St. Peter's denial of Christ, and how his being forgiven was a sign of God's mercy, His understanding of human nature. Total crap. I turned it in, got it approved, then sat down and wrote out a different homily to deliver—one that stood no chance of getting approved, naturally. The only kind of homily I wanted to be associated with.

Δ

The first thing I noticed when I got up to speak next morning was that there were no Fathers in chapel. A lucky break! I started in on a real fire-and-brimstone number, all about the emptiness and worthlessness of the sacrament of Confession. How every act of Confession was an act of hypocrisy, how Confession as we practiced it in our time was itself a sin—a lie to ourselves, to God. How it was not possible for us to sincerely repent for our sins, that we could never put the fear of damnation out of our minds and care only about how we had wounded God, as was required for true forgiveness, and that the very fact that we knew we could wipe the slate clean by going to Confession only served to make us feel safer in sinning.

And on and on and on…it was quite a show. About halfway through, I saw freshmen looking around in a panic for one of the Fathers.

Δ

Father Mario came to second period—Latin class—to call me out and bring me down to Father Harris's office. "You stirred up another hornet's nest," he said as he led me down the hall.

The meeting was brief. "We've called your parents and told them that you'll be going home tomorrow. You are to pack your things today, get ready to leave, and we'll be taking you to the airport at nine in the morning. Your parents have already purchased your ticket. We'd like you to leave with as little fuss as possible." He didn't bother to explain why I was leaving—I knew I'd sealed my doom with that last act of defiance.

All I could think was how quickly they'd done everything. For the rest, I just felt numb, disbelieving. Horrified at what he must have told my parents. Shocked—for some reason, I didn't think they'd actually kick me out.

And beginning to understand that I'd basically forced the Fathers to do what I couldn't bring myself to do—get me to leave, to go home, to get on with my life, to stop hiding.

Δ

There turned out to be something of an informal ritual at St. Anthony's for departures like mine. Fellow seminarians would gather around the bed of the expellee and sit there talking and eating snacks far into the night. I had a crowd of fifteen or so sitting around with me, watching me pack, talking about everything except the fact that I was leaving.

I'd spent a lot of time imagining what it must be like to be kicked out of the seminary. Something along the lines of Adam and Eve being expelled from the Garden of Eden. But this was a real dud from the drama standpoint. It wasn't anywhere near as big a deal as I'd pictured it being. Aside from dreading having to face my parents, who I figured were in a profound state of shock, I wasn't as upset as I'd expected to be in a situation like this. I just felt numb.

Δ

In the morning, I felt a little like someone waking up on the morning of his execution. I got my luggage together and made my way down to the turnaround at the top of the road leading off the grounds, to wait for the Father who'd drive me to the airport. A couple of classmates helped bring my bags down.

I was a little surprised to see how many people were down there waiting to see me off—it seemed like the whole student body, practically. Not the norm. We all just stood around, no one saying anything except for a few of the guys coming up to shake hands and say goodbye. Every time I looked up at the others, they all looked terribly mournful—exactly how I was feeling.

Father Ochiltree drove up and helped put my luggage in the trunk. Then he got in the car and waited for me to get in.

I shook hands with a few more guys, then couldn't figure out what to do next, how to turn away gracefully and coolly get in the car.

And then I just burst out bawling.

△

I was horrified. What was going on with me? It was embarrassing, crying like that in front of everybody. Especially since I knew that this is what I'd secretly wanted—that I had forced the Fathers to send me home because I couldn't pull the trigger myself. And I wasn't supposed to give a shit about anything the Fathers did to me. So this was uncool, to say the least.

But I was helpless—I just couldn't get myself to stop.

I could see confusion and embarrassment on the faces of everyone else. The whole exit, which I should have managed with a few choice wisecracks, had turned into a mortifying fiasco. It was obvious that everybody was embarrassed for me, and disappointed as well. I should have been walking out in style, defiant, triumphant, like Murray Burns, leaving a bunch of humiliated Fathers behind, gnashing their teeth in frustration.

Instead, the humiliation was all mine—the Fathers had won.

△

I got in the car and rode off to the airport, sobbing, trying mightily to stop, just completely helpless. Father

Ochiltree drove in silence, and sat in silence with me at the airport, neither of us saying a word, me just sniffling constantly, until the time came at last for me to board.

61

I waited until everyone else was off the plane, then walked out to face my parents, who both looked stricken. This was an unusual look for my dad, who generally just looked furious when I was in any kind of distress.

Δ

We didn't do much talking on the two-hour drive home. And when we walked in the door, my dad had me sit down immediately in the kitchen so he could give me a haircut. I got the traditional family buzz cut...very Marine Corps. And a clear message from the Old Man that he was still in charge when it came to me and my pretensions to rebellion. No more of the kind of coddling I'd been getting from those priests.

Δ

As soon as he was finished, I went up to my bedroom and lay face down on the bed, hoping never to have to get up.

I heard my mother come up the stairs and into the room. "I just want to make sure you to understand," she said, "that no one has to know what happened—why you had to leave. As far as other people are concerned, you just decided to come home."

Thirty-five years later, at a family Thanksgiving, I would be drinking with my three brothers when I would

Fred Moody

refer to some family event as having happened "the year I got kicked out of the seminary." They would stare at me in shock before one of them would gather his wits enough to say, "You got *kicked out*? We thought you just wanted to come home!"

62

It was heartbreaking to see how excited my mother was at my high-school graduation ceremony, which I had desperately hoped to avoid. She was so giddy you've have thought I'd had four splendid years at Bellingham High, instead of a mere five months, and that I was graduating in the normal fashion.

I walked through the ceremony for her sake, making no effort to look celebratory. Afterward, watching class-mates—kids I'd gone to grade school with but who now didn't seem to recognize or remember me—hugging, crying, remembering, bonding, I felt dead inside.

Δ

A few months into my first college term, I decided to cease practicing my last—vestigial—bit of external piety: attendance at Sunday Mass. I also decided to tell my moth-er about this momentous decision.

She didn't take it well. She looked crushed, in fact—even worse than she'd looked when I got off the plane from St. Anthony's. But she didn't say anything.

A hour or so later, when she walked past where I was sitting, I asked her what time it was. "I don't know," she answered. "I don't know anything anymore!"

Δ

My first two years of college were spent in a drug-

Fred Moody

and alcohol-delivered haze that seemed more complicated than simple oblivion. That is what occurred to me, at any rate, when my friend Willie Cunningham, a companion on countless drunken binges and acid trips, took me aside one morning and said, "I know we're all doing too many drugs and shit, but what you're doing is different—it's scary."

Δ

Weirdly enough, people seemed drawn to me during those years, for reasons I generally assumed to be problematic, in that they either suffered from terrible judgment or were up to something unsavory.

Mostly, I noticed a tendency on my part to bring out the inner pedophile in people. My first sexual explorations were with an older woman, my boss. And I was taken under the wing of a science professor at school, a bachelor, who was to come out years later. We went off into the Mt. Baker National Forest one afternoon to drop acid and soak in a hot spring. We were three hours or so into that trip, the acid rush humming along nicely, when his voice turned caring, concerned, intimate, and he said, "You're always so guarded. Why don't you ever tell anyone about yourself?"

"What do you mean?"

"I mean, I'd like to know a little about the natural history of Fred Moody."

"There's nothing natural about my history!"

Now he was really interested. "Why do you say that?"

I had no idea what was behind his little attempt at intimacy, but I definitely didn't like the vibe. The Marioesque way he was hovering over me. I didn't answer that last question, and the sounds of my silence made him back off.

I could tell that my sudden unreasoning rage scared the living shit out of him—something that happened on every one of those rare occasions when my temper would fly out of control. I had a way of suddenly snapping at people that made them shut the fuck up.

It was my "No nice girl would want to go out with me" voice; the words in themselves weren't all that remarkable, but the tone sent people packing.

Δ

It was only recently that I came to understand that three-year passage—long stretches of drug- and drink-delivered oblivion lit by flashes of anger—as a classic born-again experience, the same clichéd trajectory as that traversed during the rebirth of fundamentalist Christians: wandering in the wilderness, beset by cluelessness, degradation, self-loathing, ending up stoned and/or drunk face-down in the mud, finally crawling back up and reaching redemption. Emerging as a newly born, newly blessed person.

63

Born again, in adulthood, I felt bracingly sane. Grateful every day for my undeserved good fortune.

But it was a complicated sanity—a normal married life, with an astonishing wife and astonishing children, and this secret dark little gnome gnawing away at my heart.

Other people have an Inner Child; I got stuck with an Inner Monster.

I don't know that I was all that aware of the IM until I had children—adorable daughters, each of them the soul of sweetness. I found during their toddlerhood that their innocence, their vulnerability, their helplessness, their utter dependence on me, their unconditional love for me… it tended to inspire terrible rage.

Δ

Which I managed to suppress. When I tell them now that I remember and rue being an impatient father with a tendency to lose his temper with them, they just laugh.

But even though they didn't necessarily see it, or don't remember it now, it was definitely there, the temper, secretly roaring in my heart.

Δ

My current theory: that their innocence, their

infinite faith in me, brought back the memory of my being similarly in thrall to my surrogate parents at St. Anthony's, who turned out to be monsters.

Not that I understood any of this when confronted with my daughters—all I knew then is that my monstrous reaction to their sweetness, their helplessness, was wrong, wrong, wrong.

Δ

But then I was carrying this terrible secret around with me as well. About my last encounter with Father Mario.

64

It happened in the middle of the night before I was sent home the next morning. I was on my way off the grounds, making a final Midnight Mail Service delivery, when Mario emerged from behind the infirmary. He saw me walking by with a handful of letters and jumped out in front of me.

It was only in retrospect—after reading the reports about his abuse—that I understood his behavior then. At the time, I couldn't figure out why he was so agitated. But now I realize that he saw me carrying letters and immediately figured out that I was helping other kids—some of whom may have been victims—avoid his censorship.

He blocked my way. "What are you doing?"

"What difference does it make now?"

"What have you got there?"

Before I could answer, he tried to grab the letters and ended up with a grip on my arm. At which point I slugged him with my free hand, my fist, and sent him reeling. And then the Rage came down, and I more or less blacked out.

What I remember next is getting him up and over the little wall, hearing him go tumbling down into the canyon. Then I picked up the letters, took off, made my delivery, came back, and cleaned myself up.

Δ

As for what happened after that, I don't know. I got up next morning, made my disgraceful and embarrassing exit, and never had any further contact with anyone at the seminary.

I never really understood where that rage—that superhuman strength—came from, until I read those reports and recognized some of the victims. Friends of mine, including Tommy Davis, whom I'd been asked to protect. I realized that some part of me had to have been aware of what Father Mario was doing—some subconscious agent that reacted appropriately that night. I think now about all the things going on around me that my conscious mind turned away from, and how my conscience surely could only tolerate so much evasion.

Δ

Forever after, I've expected police to show up at my door. A constant state of secret panic while I busily set about building a normal-seeming life for myself.

But of course now I can see that there was no need to worry. Obviously, no one at St. Anthony's wanted police agencies or anyone else from the outside poking into Father Mario's life.

The Franciscans hadn't called anyone's attention to his disappearance at the time for reasons that became obvious when the scandal finally broke. I mean, Father Xavier and the rest of them knew perfectly well what he was doing—it's easy to see why they didn't want to involve the police in his disappearance, and just as easy to see how no one outside the walls knew anything about him.

Δ

Over the years, I came to accept that no one was going to come looking for me or connecting me to Father Mario's death. But I never got over what I'd done—even though, truth be told, it was a good rather than a bad deed. I mean, God only knows how many victims I preemptively spared. How could anyone call what I'd done a crime?

Δ

Still. When I was immersed in these reports, in these memories, in this writing exercise, there was another fire in the area around St. Anthony's, another inferno in that canyon. And this time, they did have to evacuate the grounds, and this time the flames did come up the St. Anthony's side, burned away all the vegetation, and uncovered human skeletal remains. How hard would it be to figure out whose they were, and what happened? And how long before police came up here to talk with me?

Exomologesis

Novelists get a free ride, presenting fact as fiction and taking undeserved credit for creativity when they've simply taken down what reality dictated to them. But let a nonfiction writer try to present fiction as fact for the noble cause of inspiring and uplifting the reader, and he ends up crucified on *Oprah*.

Δ

I kept my mind closed to my past for as long as I could. It took seventeen years from when the scandal broke—forty-four years from the day I left—for me to work up the will to properly revisit my seminary days. It didn't take much searching to find detailed reporting on the abuse scandal, and particularly on Father Mario and his protectors. And even though I can claim not to have known at the time—can say that it simply wasn't possible in that uniquely Catholic climate of repression to imagine the unimaginable—I still have to confess that I wasn't at all surprised by the findings on Father Mario.

Δ

A friar had a practice of calling students to his room to conduct "hernia examinations" (despite the fact that the students had undergone legitimate physical examinations by licensed physicians prior to coming to the seminary). The friar instructed the students to entirely disrobe. His "examination" included handling the students' genitals.

Δ

Another student was called by this friar to his room on several occasions for the purpose of having his genital hygiene checked. Each time, in spite of the fact that the student was diligently keeping himself clean, the student's genitals were examined, washed and dried by the friar. Thereafter, on three additional occasions, the friar had the student come to his room and take a shower; the friar then showed him pornography and had him lie down naked on the friar's bed. The friar proceeded to masturbate and orally copulate the student, who attempted to avoid becoming aroused. After each incident, the friar warned the student to keep the abuse secret under threat of expulsion from the seminary.

Δ

Cimmarrusti would order students to his room to conduct supposed hernia exams. Fr. Cimmarrusti assaulted Victim #14 (Class of '68) numerous times during these "hernia exams." Cimmarrusti repeatedly sexually assaulted Victim #14 under the pretense of conducting a medical examination. These faux exams were done for Fr. Cimmarrusti's own sexual gratification as Cimmarrusti had no medical training and no legitimate basis, reason, authority or right to conduct any such exam or to even touch Victim #14 or any other student. According to Victim #15, Fr. Cimmarrusti conducted so-called hernia exams of every freshman at least three to four times a month. Victim #15 recalls the assaults taking place in the infirmary, in Cimmarrusti's office, and at least once in the changing room of the pool at the Mission. With another student, Victim #16 (Class of '71), Cimmarrusti took advantage of Victim #16 developing a case of athlete's foot and used it as an excuse to assault Victim #16 on

the ridiculous grounds he was making sure it (athlete's foot) had
not spread to Victim #16's genitals.

Δ

It's hard to know what was worse for me now: taking in the sheer scope of the abuse that had been going on while I was there, or recognizing fellow seminarians, pawns/pebbles in Father Mario's game, some of them friends, one of them a friend left in my charge, among the victims in these reports. Realizing that they were being assaulted and I did nothing, and that they didn't feel they could come to me for help.

Δ

John Doe 39, a 54-year-old Washington state resident
who came to St. Anthony's as a sophomore in 1966, claims the
Rev. Cimmarrusti fondled him during medical exams, mas-
turbated him and showed him pornography, among other more
serious acts of sexual misconduct, according to documents, and
interviews with his lawyers. The physical and sexual abuse was
so bad that he ran away and sneaked onto a plane at Los Ange-
les International Airport, according to court papers. He says in
his lawsuit that he told at least two administrators about what
was happening—a claim that will be contested in court.

Δ

Cimmarrusti ordered Victim #12 to Cimmarrusti's
room to receive punishment for misconduct fabricated by Cim-
marrusti which Victim #12 did not commit. Once there, Cim-
marrusti ordered Victim #12 to strip naked from the waist
down, and bent Victim #12 over Cimmarrusti's lap as Cim-

marrusti sat in his chair. Cimmarrusti then violently beat/ spanked Victim #12's naked buttocks/upper thighs over a period of approximately fifteen to twenty minutes. Cimmarrusti struck Victim #12 with such force, approximately fifteen to twenty-five times, that by the end of each beating his buttocks/upper thighs were black and blue. Throughout the beating, Fr. Cimmarrusti was sexually aroused and Victim #12 could feel Cimmarrusti's erection. Additionally, with each blow Victim #12 cried and screamed in pain with such volume other priests, faculty and students had to have known what was taking place. In fact, Victim #12 himself recalls hearing Fr. Cimmarrusti beat Victim #19 in Cimmarrusti's room, and recalls being able to hear each of Cimmarrusti's blows and Victim #19's screams of pain. Cimmarrusti's beating of Victim #19 lasted for approximately ten minutes. So loud were 1) the screams by Victim #19 and 2) Fr. Cimmarrusti's blows that Victim #12 was able to hear both from the St Anthony's parking lot. Any claim by Defendants that they or their agents were unaware of the abuse taking place is preposterous.

Δ

Victim #15 also was sexually assaulted and beaten by Cimmarrusti so badly he bruised like Victim #12 and also bled from his wounds. Victim #15 recalls Fr. Cimmarrusti requiring him to strip completely naked during one of the beatings, and then proceeding to strike Victim #15 thirty-three times, "once for each year of our Lord's life." During these beatings Victim #15 could feel Fr. Cimmarrusti's erection. Victim #15 also recalls the entire school was aware of the beatings. After the beatings, Cimmarrusti had the sobbing victims drop to their knees; caressed, stroked and blessed them while pulling their heads into his crotch; and frequently threatened them with eternal damnation if they told anyone.

Fred Moody

△

Victim #9 went to St. Anthony's rector, Xavier Harris, and reported the attempted rape by Cimmarrusti. Fr. Harris responded promptly by questioning Victim #9's "vocation" and expelling him from St. Anthony's. Meanwhile, Fr. Cimmarrusti's abuse of St. Anthony's students continued. Id.

During that same year, 1965, Victim #22 recalls being sexually assaulted by Cimmarrusti in Cimmarrusti's room and seeing another priest come to Cimmarrusti's door in a position to see Victim #22 on Cimmarrusti's bed. Approximately one year later in 1966, Victim #22 also reported to Fr. Harris the weekly beatings and sexual abuse he was receiving from Fr. Cimmarrusti, and told Harris he could not take it any more and wanted to leave St. Anthony's. Fr. Harris first told Victim #22 he had imagined the abuse. When Victim #22 insisted the abuse had happened and that he wished to drop out of school, Fr. Harris offered to make him, among other things, class president and captain of the football team if Victim #22 agreed to stay. When Victim #22 still refused, Fr. Harris threatened to report this to Victim #22's very traditional Catholic family. He reminded Victim #22 he would be seen as a quitter and a failure, and that his family would be ostracized as they lived in a small town and everyone would know. He told Victim #22 this would eventually lead to his parents' divorce and that this would be Victim #22's fault. Victim #22 still insisted on, and ultimately did, leave St. Anthony's.

△

Additionally, in approximately 1967-68, Fr. Gino Piccoli walked in on Fr. Cimmarrusti orally copulating yet another victim, had a clear view of the abuse, and turned around and walked out. Fr. Piccoli and Defendants took no action against Fr. Cimmarrusti, and Cimmarrusti's abuse of students continued. Years later, when a member of the laity told Fr. Piccoli of Victim #14's anger at Fr. Cimmarrusti, Fr. Piccoli responded by attacking Victim #14's credibility and stating Victim #14 should not be believed because he was severely mentally disturbed.

Δ

Fr. Cimmarrusti's abuse of St. Anthony's students spanned most of the 1960s, and could and should have been stopped by Defendants' agents at least as early as 1965. Instead, they allowed him to become one of the most prolific abusers of children in Santa Barbara County, with no less than sixteen (16) of his victims identified to date. There can be no denying the Defendants were well aware of the risk of childhood sexual abuse any child faced when exposed to their agents. By concealing the threat posed by, among others, Fr. Cimmarrusti, Defendants continued and fostered a public nuisance which placed children in Santa Barbara County at great risk to be sexually assaulted.

Δ

Franciscan School of Theology
Faculty
Xavier Harris, O.F.M.
Professor of Moral Theology (retired)

Degrees
      Ph.D. University of Notre Dame
      M.Div. Franciscan School of Theolog
      B.A. San Luis Rey College

"After almost half a century of teaching, I enjoyed the class-room more than ever. I found the students here both challenged and challenging. My goal was to share not only my knowledge but my faith. For me, theology and ministry are inseparable and mutually reinforcing."

With infinite wisdom and consummate teaching skills, Xavier's classes in ethics, virtues, and philosophy educated students not only about the ways of the world, but about the way of their own hearts.

Δ

This is what I can't get over: The shame over my complicity in that series of monstrous crimes. There's no other word for it but "complicity," my means of navigating through that year with my blinders firmly in place. I had to have been able to see what was going on—*had* to have—but I refused to acknowledge it, even to imagine it. We all did—hundreds of us, seminarians and priests alike. We aided and abetted Mario and his fellow monsters, year after year after year after year, by refusing to admit to ourselves what it was we were seeing. It wasn't just Father Harris and the other Friars who were "concealing the threat posed" by Father Mario. We were there too, all of us, watching it unfold, standing in the parking lot under that window…and we allowed ourselves to do nothing, to understand nothing. Our sin left Father Mario's crimes undiscovered until after their statute of limitations had expired, allowing him to live out his days in a comfortable retreat house home in Danville, California, denying his crimes to the end.

And more to the point: Our sin allowed the molestation to continue for decades, not only in Santa Barbara but throughout the worldwide Catholic Church. Thousands of victims through the second half of the twentieth century, each one of whom might have been spared if I'd spoken out then. For it is inarguable now that conditions in the institutional Catholic Church—that swamp of repression, secrecy and shame—were ideal for nurturing molesters. Who still—still!—roam among us, and will continue to do so until the Church itself, all of it, is brought down. Someone—i.e., I—should have had the courage and imagination to understand what he was witnessing back in the day, and put an end to it.

Δ

And even now, in 2013, well after the word got out, we persist in whitening the sepulchre, pretending that the molesters never existed, that we never abetted them.

Along with the material I dredged up in these reports I found a celebratory web site for St. Anthony's alums. Consider this prose on its History page, written by someone who was there with me when Father Mario was having his way with our friends back in the day:

For more than 90 years, the Franciscan Friars fostered the creation of community at Saint Anthony's Seminary. From it's [sic] roots at Old Mission Santa Barbara in 1896, until it's [sic] final senior graduation in 1987, about 4000 young men passed through the halls of Saint Anthony's! Some stayed for only a few months while others stayed until they graduated; but all experienced the life and the love of Saint Francis of Assisi.

Postscript

In 1999, I took my friend Billy Joe, a Methodist, to the old seminary grounds one day when we were in Santa Barbara on a business trip. It was the first time I'd been back.

It was a foggy day—really foggy—which only served to enhance the creepy spirituality of the place. We walked along the covered walkway beside the study hall and classrooms, toward the chapel, and through the fog we could hear a boys' choir singing. Way down at the end of the walkway, at the entrance to the chapel, in this swirling fog, we could see a friar standing there, in profile, in his hooded robe.

It was positively archetypal. Billy Joe, a student of religious history, started hyperventilating. When we got up to the friar, he greeted us courteously and we answered in kind. But I could see Billy Joe staring at him in horror. With those young boys' beautiful high voices filling the air, we looked at this monk in the swirling mist, his face ravaged with the telltale signs of alcoholism: the big red potato for a nose, prominent veins running all over his face, the rheumy eyes.... He was the picture of dissipation, rot, the ravages of sin. How could he—his kind, his ilk—still be living their accustomed comfortable lives, still be respected, even revered, after all the publicity about the savagery his fellow monks were known to have wreaked in this place?

Δ

I took Billy Joe down through a maze of stone-walled paths until we ended up at a huge ornate metal gate in an interior courtyard. We were having a high old time, me regaling him with horror stories while we snapped picture after picture of the place.

I stepped through that gate, closed it, and turned and faced Billy Joe with my hands gripping the bars, as if trying to tear the gate loose so I could break free. Billy Joe took a picture that turned out to have a perfect tone to it: spooky, dim, a little scary, my backlit figure with its hands overhead, gripping those bars in that misty air.

We entitled it "Prisoner of Memory." Then we got the hell out of there.

Made in the USA
San Bernardino, CA
01 October 2013